Barbo

Your audience will really love this message

"Customers must take action to get the service they deserve. The Customer Is Boss is a quality guide that shows consumers how to get good customer service every time."

GERRI DETWEILER
EXECUTIVE DIRECTOR, BANKCARD HOLDERS OF AMERICA

"The voice of the consumer has never been more powerful than in today's competitive and complex global market. Businesses know that if they are to succeed, then they must be able to react to the consumer's needs. In The Customer Is Boss, John Tschohl offers a road map, detailing how consumers can let businesses know the quality they expect in services and products."

ELIZABETH DOLE
FORMER UNITED STATES SECRETARY OF LABOR

"A simple, no nonsense book that can definitely help the frustrated consumer who isn't getting the satisfaction they deserve from a product or service."

JEAN M. OTTE
PRESIDENT, SOCIETY OF CUSTOMER AFFAIRS PROFESSIONALS
VICE PRESIDENT, QUALITY ASSURANCE NATIONAL CAR RENTAL

"John Tschohl has done a great service for the average under-serviced consumer. Here is the true art of complaining — how to, who to, when to — with practically guaranteed results."

JERRY NOACK
PUBLISHER, TRAINING MAGAZINE

"A bill of rights and a guide to action for customers; contains thought provoking ideas for business managers."

DR. WILLIAM BYHAM
CEO, DEVELOPMENT DIMENSIONS INTERNATIONAL
CO-AUTHOR, ZAPP

"The Customer Is Boss is a helpful guide for taking care of your most valuable asset — your customers."

KEN BLANCHARD
CO-AUTHOR, THE ONE MINUTE MANAGER

"The Customer Is Boss is a treasure chest of practical information about earning good service. I highly endorse the strategies in John Tschohl's excellent book!"

PAUL J. MEYER
FOUNDER, SUCCESS MOTIVATION INSTITUTE, INC. AND LEADERSHIP MANAGEMENT, INC.

"John Tschohl has done it again! Now the consumer has a personal handbook to guarantee receiving excellent service from store clerks to attorneys; every quality conscious owner and manager should have their customers read this book."

DR. ROBERT E. HUNTER
PRESIDENT, DELTA DENTAL PLAN OF MASSACHUSETTS

"Excellent book — John Tschohl has included not only the what but also the how — the 'how' to get good service. I know what good service looks like. This book will help me get more of it."

AL WALKER, CSP, CPAE
PRESIDENT, NATIONAL SPEAKERS ASSOCIATION

"The 'customer' movement in business is now reaching even the most resistant pockets of government. But it won't be complete anywhere until paying customers demand all the quality and efficiency they deserve. Tschohl tells them how."

ARNE CARLSON
GOVERNOR OF MINNESOTA

"A refreshing approach to handling service invitations. We, in business, need constructive feedback to give better service."

ROBERT GANDRUD
PRESIDENT, LUTHERAN BROTHERHOOD

"An educated consumer that lets us know our strengths and weaknesses is our greatest ally in our quest for total customer satisfaction."

GARY PAXTON
PRESIDENT, DOLLAR SYSTEMS

"The Customer Is Boss will help consumers fight back against the all too frequent product and service abuses they suffer. John Tschohl offers practical steps for both registering a complaint and getting satisfaction. The price of the book will be repaid many times over by the savings it will render."

RICHARD C. WHITELY
VICE PRESIDENT, THE FORUM CORPORATION,
AUTHOR, THE CUSTOMER — DRIVEN COMPANY

"This book is very concrete and realistic, especially in Russia. I greatly appreciate it."

OLEG URALOV
PRESIDENT, VIDEOFILM CORPORATION, RUSSIA

"I sincerely believe that The Customer Is Boss is one of the finest books ever written in the important, and greatly neglected field of customer service. It's entertaining enough to make it digestible and the powerful principles are presented withthe divinity of simplicity. Don't pass up the opportunity to absorb these fabulous ideas."

CAVETT ROBERT

"Tschohl does it again...with clarity of purpose and simply-stated logic, he's created the consumers' "Bill of Rights" when it comes to better customer service. Yes, quality service is attainable, and The Customer Is Boss is the initiative that can make it happen!"

BERNIE TRACHTENBERG
PUBLISHER, HUMAN RESOURCE EXECUTIVE MAGAZINE

"This book is very useful for all people in Russia. I support the ideas and practice proposed in this book."

MIKHAIL KABATTCHENKO, ED.D.
CHAIRMAN, EDUCATORS FOR PEACE AND UNDERSTANDING IN RUSSIA

"Many books are written for bosses on how to provide good service. This does not guarantee excellent service for the customer. Now John Tschohl gives the customer the tolls to get superior service — a unique and important difference. It returns control back to the customer, who really is the boss."

LAURA LISWOOD
AUTHOR, SERVING THEM RIGHT

"John Tschohl's excellent book motivates us, in business, to do an even better job in serving our customers to their complete satisfaction."

THOMAS MEINL
PRESIDENT, JULIUS MEINL, AUSTRIA

"At last — a book that helps the consumer recognize their privilege of good service and their responsibility to reward those who give it by their business! Again, John Tschohl has provided an excellent format and increased customer satisfaction."

NAOMI RHODE CSP, CPAE
PRESIDENT ELECT, NATIONAL SPEAKERS ASSOCIATION

"John Tschohl's new book is a primer for every buyer — and seller. Customer service pays huge dividends and customers who are persistent, firm and reasonable will get their way. The Customer Is Boss tells them how."

RUDY BOSCHWITZ
UNITED STATES SENATE
CHAIRMAN, HOME VALU

"A practical blueprint for solving problems."

DEE J. ATKINSON
GOVERNMENT AND INDUSTRY AFFAIRS OFFICER,
KEMPER NATIONAL INSURANCE COMPANIES

"In Brazil, every consumer should read this book to really understand why The Customer Is Boss."

ANDRE PALO HERMANN
TDC, BRAZIL

"John Tschohl's titles make you think,
his examples make you feel
and his logic makes you agree...
But, it is his concept that makes you act!
The Customer Is Boss is a quick read
with workable ideas."

PAUL C. GREEN, PH.D.
INDUSTRIAL ORGANIZATIONAL PSYCHOLOGIST

"A wonderful A to Z game plan on how to demand good service, just what the buying public needs. This fast-read book is a 'must read' for us all. Thank you John Tschohl for championing the fight-back crusade. No more caveat emptor (let the buyer beware). Now Tschohl is to be saluted for showing us how to be aware of good service and bad service, and how to address the latter."

PATRICIA COLEMAN
VICE PRESIDENT/ASSOCIATE PUBLISHER, BUILDING SUPPLY HOME CENTERS

"Must read! Tschohl tells you how to create happy customers. This book is going into our manager's success library at Stew's."

STEW LEONARD
PRESIDENT, STEW LEONARD'S

"I found John Tschohl's new book really helpful in transmitting the idea of 'the customer is first' to people working directly with students in my University. I strongly recommend it for customer service seminars and courses."

ALVERO CASTRO HARRIGAN
RECTOR ULACIT, UNIVERSIDAD LATINOAMERICANA, COSTA RICA

"Everyone has received poor customer service at one time or another. In The Customer Is Boss, my friend John Tschohl teaches consumers how to change poor customer service into the quality customer service they deserve."

BILL MACK
SCULPTOR

THE CUSTOMER IS BOSS

A PRACTICAL GUIDE FOR GETTING WHAT YOU PAID FOR AND MORE

John Tschohl

 For information address Best Sellers Publishing, 9201 East Bloomington Freeway, Minneapolis, MN 55420. Phone: (612) 888-7672 and Fax: (612) 884-8901

Publisher's Cataloging-In-Publication Data

Tschohl, John.

The customer is boss: a practical guide for getting what you paid for and more / by John Tschohl.

p. cm.

ISBN 0-9636268-0-9

1. Customer Service. I. Title.

HF5415.5.T 1993

381.33 — dc20 92-076103

CIP

Table of Contents

ACKNOWLEDGEMENTS

My special thanks go to Hazel Brown, who has been my assistant for more than 19 years, and to Steve Franzmeier, who assisted me in the writing of this book and who co-authored my other book, *Achieving Excellence Through Customer Service.*

The job that is too difficult for Hazel has not yet been invented.

Steve coordinated the communication program for Service Quality Institute for some seven years. During that time he managed to persuade hundreds of trade and business magazine editors, syndicated writers, general interest magazine editors, electronic media program directors and others that the articles and news stories that he submitted to them were worthy of their media.

My Service Quality Institute staff — every one of them — has been extremely cooperative in obtaining information requested from them and in validating details.

To my wife, Pat, and to my children, Christina and Matthew, "Thank you" for tolerating my obsession with excellence in customer service.

Preface

SOLUTION TO BAD SERVICE: COOPERATION

"It's a shame, but in America today when we get good service we are surprised by it. People don't expect it, they don't demand it, and they settle for a lot less than they should."

— F. G. (Buck) Rodgers
Former Corporate Vice President of Marketing, IBM

For the past 12 years I have been teaching businesses how to *provide* quality service.

During that time I learned that a true service-oriented culture in America is possible only when...

1. consumers know what they can do to obtain quality service; and,

2. when business is motivated to provide quality service.

Business must offer good service to consumers who are determined to both prevent and *reject* bad service. Only then will our economy achieve the service ideal sought by most people.

No matter what your problem, no matter what your complaint, you, the consumer, can gain satisfaction in the marketplace if you refuse to accept service that doesn't meet your needs or desires in terms of promptness, courtesy, convenience, product knowledge, and the ability to actually solve your problem. You need no longer feel that you are doomed to be a victim the rest of your consuming life.

When you follow the simple guidelines in this book, you will gain better service in department stores, in restaurants, and in supermarkets.

You will experience a boost in the respect shown you by professionals such as physicians, dentists and attorneys.

You will feel secure and fearless in the knowledge that if you purchase a product that fails through no fault of your own, it will be repaired or replaced to your satisfaction.

What is my justification for making this promise to you?

Over the years I have worked with thousands of people called "consumers." I've learned why salespeople and others in service positions treat you poorly and what you can do to...

1. prevent bad service; or,

2. to change bad service to good service.

I have come to know not only the frustrations of consumers but the causes of poor service by some businesses.

I will teach you methods that have been effective for men and women just like yourself in big cities, small towns, and places in between.

This book is dedicated to the principle that consumers *and* business benefit when consumers demand good service in a reasonable manner and when they exercise informed and effective criticism of bad service in this service economy.

A loud, table-pounding, threatening approach is uncalled for. It's also counterproductive because, instead of encouraging an openness to listening and a desire to solve your problem, this approach puts the person on the defensive and closes out any possible chance for having a constructive, problem-solving dialogue.

The problem of bad service can be solved through *cooperation* between consumers, on the one hand, and business, government, and private organizations on the other.

We hope that this book will promote reasoned cooperation through which much more will be achieved than could be done through confrontation.

This book shows you how to challenge bad service in a calm, reasoned, effective manner. You must be as fair as you want business to be. It's easier for you to feel that you are justified in complaining if you complain for the right reasons, one of which is *not* "revenge."

Remember that friendliness *with* salespeople has a way of begetting friendliness (and good service) *by* salespeople.

So, read on. Read on and discover that complaining can be an honorable avocation if you do it constructively and for legitimate reasons.

Read on and learn that you are *not* helpless in the marketplace.

You, as an *individual*, have *power* — power to *fight back* and to improve service for yourself and for other consumers who have tolerated rotten service far too long.

INTRODUCTION

"Personal service has become
a maddeningly rare commodity in the marketplace...
customers know service when they miss it,
and now they want it back."

— TIME MAGAZINE

Good service is as much the responsibility of consumers as it is of businesses.

Consider this reasoning: A business cannot correct a service deficiency until it is aware that a deficiency exists. Complaints by customers often are the first hint for a business that its employees are alienating customers, working at cross-purposes with management.

If supervisors had their way, every customer would feel complete satisfaction so that they would return to buy again. But, supervisors can't stand around and watch their service employees at work all day.

Here's where *you* come in.

Too many of us have accepted bad service as a normal part of everyday life. But, it should be an exception, not the rule.

This book points out that you, as a consumer, also have a responsibility — at least to yourself. You must call bad service to the attention of managers, supervisors, owners and others to whom front-line service employees report.

The message in this book is: You *can* obtain redress for wrongs visited upon you by those businesses interested only in the shortest or fastest route to your wallet and who feel they can't be bothered to provide service *also.*

You *can* obtain satisfaction for insulting treatment by salespeople and by clerks who consider you, the customer, to be an unwelcome interruption in an otherwise pleasant day.

So, consumers must "complain"...constructively. Complain *before* dissatisfaction degenerates into anger.

Don't *ever* feel guilty about complaining. You deserve good service. You *pay for good service.*

When a business gives you surly service, don't ever excuse it. After all, it costs business nothing extra to be friendly... unless you consider the cost of persuading employees that they should provide service and showing them how to do it.

We urge you *now* to resolve *never* to accept insults or indifference by people you're buying from.

Fight back! *Resign* from the silent majority.

Every time you let bad service go by without objecting, you're encouraging it. You're rewarding employees for being lazy. You're making it acceptable for them to not be interested in doing a good job.

Do not ever allow an outrage or an oversight to slip by without telling a service person about it. If they do not apologize or correct a problem, then tell their supervisors, too.

Every time you tip a waitperson who didn't notice you for 20 minutes and then brought your steak well done instead of medium rare, as you ordered it, you encourage a repeat performance for unsuspecting future customers. You should instead complain to the waitperson's supervisor.

Things have gotten so bad that service workers expect tips no matter how rotten the service they provide...or *don't* provide.

Said a Japanese visitor to America, Tadashi Nishimura of Osaka: "I don't mind tipping, but services I got in America were so bad that on a number of occasions I could not reward them with money. Yet, you are more or less forced to tip everywhere you go."

In a business environment that is becoming more impersonal and automated than ever before, you *must* complain. Or, you will continue to get bad service and suffer frustration in the form of splitting headaches, upset stomachs and brooding anger.

Complaining is appropriate and *necessary*.

BENEFITS OF FIGHTING BACK

There is solace for the spirit in fighting back. There is satisfaction in winning fair treatment when all around you consumers are shaking their heads and grinding their teeth.

So, following the guidelines in this book for claiming the service that you pay for *pays off*.

This book tells you *how to* fight back. It shows you *how to* strike a blow for service. It shows you *how to* get together with other consumers to bring stronger pressure to bear upon reluctant businesses and their staffs.

One way that consumers can influence business to provide good service is to educate business owners and managers to the fact that a proper service attitude and satisfied customers have a strong, positive impact upon the bottom line.

Some businesspeople don't realize that good service is profitable. It can be a competitive edge. It can be the only reason that they survive in bad economic times.

A good point to make to businesspeople is that they save money on new advertising and promotion when they keep more of the customers won by previous advertising and promotion.

(It costs five times as much to obtain a new customer as to keep a present customer.)

TIME magazine wrote in a cover story on customer service: "Personal service has become a maddeningly rare commodity in the marketplace...customers know service when they miss it, and now they want it back."

If you feel this way, then you should read this book.

Do rude or ignorant and indifferent service workers anger you? If so, then this book is for *you.*

Do you rage about rotten service to your friends, your spouse and your relatives but merely glare at offensive service employees?

If so, then you should read this book, by all means.

ACTION FOR SATISFACTION

This book also shows you how to *earn* good service when you make a purchase and how to obtain satisfaction when business or government agencies provide bad service.

This book shows you how to complain *effectively.* Call it "constructive criticism." Never forget that you *ought* to complain, because the cost of a purchase should pay for both the merchandise *and* the service.

Your money buys the right to respectful treatment, the right to be informed, assisted and respected — not just the right to spend your money and get the goods.

You ought to take action to win satisfaction because by doing so you help fellow consumers obtain good service in the future.

You will also be helping business. Businesspeople, after all, don't intentionally seek customer *dis*satisfaction. They don't *oppose* the notion of providing good service. But, they are often so narrowly focused upon profit that they tend to overlook service.

One company displays a large sign with the words: "We *love* it when you give us the business." With your help, more companies will adopt that philosophy.

THE BUSINESS POINT OF VIEW

"Consumers are not the only losers in the perilous world of caveat emptor (let the buyer beware), so are the companies that refuse to recognize positive benefits of responsive consumer policy."

—Jack Gillis
Consumer Federation of America

What we have in the marketplace today is a *problem.*

Business often argues that the problem is exaggerated. That's possible, but the significant point for business is that poor service is *perceived* as a problem *by consumers.*

Consumers could be wrong, but we don't think they are.

Surveys consistently show that consumers think they receive bad service — a lot of it. Their views appear in reports on surveys by leading customer service research firms, by the U.S. Office of Consumer Affairs and by corporations themselves.

THE BAD EGGS: GOOD BUSINESS REPUDIATES THEM

A separate book, a very large one, can be written about creative service strategies in business — about employee training to head off customer dissatisfaction and complaints and to resolve any unavoidable complaints to the satisfaction of customers.

Actually, I've written that book already. It's entitled *Achieving Excellence Through Customer Service* and it was published in 1991 by Prentice Hall. Throughout this book, too, we've credited business for some outstanding service achievements that, strangely, don't make the news very often.

Also, we've reminded readers that *most* businesspeople and employees of government and private organizations go out of their way to win the total satisfaction of their customers and clients.

Customer *satisfaction* is the goal of virtually every business owner. The company does not exist that wants you, the consumer, to take your business to its competitors.

Nevertheless, in the real world deficiencies do occur. These are the times that consumers can do a favor for themselves and for the business by pointing out the deficiency to the business.

Poor service often is perpetrated by fly-by-night operators, by various business scams and by underfinanced businesses so absorbed with day-to-day survival that they have no time to build a service organization. Leading companies always "take care of you" or correct a problem without question.

But, there always seem to be some businesses in "hot" fields — computers and software, environmental sanitation, vitamin therapy — that have tapped a vein of great consumer demand and then become complacent like the Cheshire cat in "Alice In Wonderland." They do a lot of business *without* providing good service.

But, eventually, their chickens come home to roost and are eaten by the Cheshire cat!

The don't-give-a-damn attitude shown by some businesses toward consumers is rejected just as vehemently by those businesses already providing good service to consumers.

Service faults usually are faults of omission. A business hasn't yet trained employees or begun a formal service program.

Or service practices have grown old and weak because they've become routine. Enthusiasm has waned. Managers don't review and reinforce service practices or demonstrate their own commitment to quality service.

Still, *most businesspeople know* that long-term customer loyalty, won with good service, is worth far more than any brief benefits gained from arranging matters for a company's convenience — and for customers' *in*convenience.

If we are to come as close as possible to the truth, we must judge each business individually. To be fair, we should not generalize...not paint all businesses with the same brush.

Remember when the employee at the insurance office sounded so friendly when you called with a question about your premium? Remember how pleased you were when you received the requested information the next day?

Remember that waitress who made you feel at home and rushed to get the extra sour cream you asked for? She deserved the big tip you left.

Remember the building supplies store salesman who carried that box of tile to your car? You could have carried it yourself.

That's *good* service. Applaud it. Tell your friends about it.

Jack Gillis, public affairs director for the Consumer Federation of America, is perceptive enough to see the wider significance of poor service: "Consumers are not the only losers in the perilous world of caveat emptor (let the buyer beware)," says Gillis. "So are the companies that refuse to recognize positive benefits of responsive consumer policy."

Most companies know it.

The story is told of Billie Burns, former men's clothing department manager at a Nordstrom department store, renowned for its good service. Burns received a call from a regular customer who was hurrying to the airport and needed some clothes. Burns gathered up a bag full of blazers, slacks, and underwear and charged them to the customer's account. He was waiting on the curb outside the store when the man's car screeched to a stop and paused just long enough for a fast exchange.

So, let's have a little recognition for those businesses in which we consistently find unfailing smiles, friendly patience, broad product knowledge, competence, alertness and enthusiasm.

CHAPTER 1

SERVICE: HOW BAD IS IT?

"This is supposed to be 'the service society.'
So where's the service?"

"We could get a lot more done around here if we didn't have all these customers bothering us."

A man who lives in a suburb of Boston wrote this plaintive account of his service experience on one very bad day:

"The dishwasher, which had been repaired on Monday, flooded the kitchen floor again. Not to worry, said the helpful person at the appliance store. Someone will be over 'between 8 a.m. and 4 p.m. Tuesday.'

"With my shoes still squishing I head to the office. But, the train is late. When it shows up there aren't enough seats and the heater has gone berserk. I want to complain, but no one answers the transit department's toll-free customer-service number.

"Things aren't any better when I finally get to work. The copier is out again; I can't get anyone at our Boston office to answer the phone; and my lunch plans go awry when the fancy French restaurant 'loses' my reservation."

Dick Youngblood, business columnist for the *Star Tribune* of Minneapolis-St. Paul, thinks that the service economy is a hoax. He lambasted "those troglodytes [anyone who lives in a primitive, low, or degenerative fashion] of the service sector who insist on keeping 9-to-5 working hours" despite the large number of families in which everybody works and nobody's home during the day.

Daytime, Youngblood points out, is the only time that many service businesses operate.

You, the reader, know how bad service is. You most likely experience bad service every day. You may have a cache of personal horror stories stored in a corner of your mind.

You've encountered problems ranging from indifferent sales clerks to rude waiters to the purchase of expensive items which not only fail to work but also seem impossible to service.

The VCR runs only in reverse, the refrigerator freezes the lettuce but not the ice cream, or a blouse labeled "Machine Washable" shrinks.

Employees act as if they think: "We could get a lot more done around here if we didn't have all these customers bothering us."

You walk into a business and you notice an employee peeking around the edge of a display rack wearing an expression that says: "Oh, cripes, here comes another one. Just when we ordered a pizza, too."

The waitress brings you a well-done steak when you ordered rare. You can't find your morning paper because it's nestled behind the bushes. Your pharmacist gives you the wrong prescription.

Your flight takes off late. Because traffic is stacked up, the plane circles...and circles. By the time you land, your baggage has been put on another plane to yet another destination.

The furniture you ordered with six-week guaranteed delivery hasn't arrived after two months.

In the supermarket, several checkout lanes stand closed while you wait in one of the open lines, moving one place forward every five minutes.

You stop after work to cash a check, or to buy something at the deli, or to pick up a gift at one of those all-purpose drug stores. The only sign of life the clerk shows is to take your money and to drop your change in your hand. She doesn't look at you, and her feeble greeting sounds more like a grunt.

We are justified in remarking: "This is supposed to be 'the service society.' So, where's the service?"

These experiences and many others are uncomfortably familiar to everyone.

People who earn their incomes providing service to customers — whose patronage pays them — should be courteous, don't you think? They should move quickly. They should be attentive and listen to you. They should be helpful and know enough about their product or service to answer questions.

This is what you deserve. This is what you should expect. And if you don't get it, you ought to let somebody know about it.

Nearly one-third of all households in America experienced at least one *significant* consumer problem during the year before, according to the National Consumer Survey (NCS) sponsored by the U.S. Office of Consumer Affairs. Of households reporting problems, more than 60 percent told of losses averaging $142.

That $142 was the sum of commercially done work such as clothes washing and drying while an appliance wasn't working, inoperable or ineffective product that was not returned for refund or exchange, cost of repair or replacement when no free repair or replacement was available and uncompensated time lost from work waiting at home for service people.

Nearly 15 percent of the problems involved lost time from work while waiting for repair people.

"We'll be there between 9 a.m. and 4 p.m.," says the very friendly service scheduler on the phone.

You ought to say: "Oh, aren't you wonderful. Will you pay me for the time I lose from work waiting for you?"

Other research supports these NCS findings. One study discovered that one out of four purchases results in a problem. A survey reported that more than 70 percent of some 100,000 respondents experienced problems with grocery products — from a bug in the jam to spoiled oranges.

This is a common variety of bad service: You stay home from work to let the plumber in and to lock up after he leaves. But the plumber doesn't show up. He doesn't call to say he won't be able to show up, either.

So you stay home a second day; and this time you lose a day's pay. Does the plumber reimburse you? Don't ask!

THIS IS A SERVICE ECONOMY?

Economists call ours a service economy. But, you'd never know it from the difficulty consumers experience in finding genuinely friendly, helpful personal service.

What consumers are getting, instead, is service people who treat them like road kill, or who seem to be "out to lunch," or who quickly disappear when they see a customer approaching.

Business Week magazine wrote: "At many department stores these days the customer isn't always right. In fact, the customer is barely tolerated."

Eric Sevareid, former CBS News commentator, believes that service in our "service economy" has worsened. That bothers him. He says: "The decline of service goes along with the decline of civility. Civility, kindness, patience with others is what makes a democratic, civilized society operate. If you forego those things, what have you got?"

Tom Peters and Nancy Austin, in their popular book *A Passion for Excellence*, point out that retailing often gives "no distinguishing service" and, as a result, has "reaped the reward — fed-up customers..."

They write: "Common decency, common courtesy...is the exception."

When Peters and Austin refer to "retailing," they really ought to say "some retailers." No doubt, most bad service is given by the same retailers over and over again. That leaves a sizable number of retailers whose names *never* show up negatively in consumer surveys.

People under 25 may never have seen a service station attendant wipe windshields except in the 1983 movie *Back to the Future*, where employees buzzed around a car with liquid glass cleaner, chamois and water can as if they were competing for a Service Attendant of the Year award.

When the media hear about a service station with service, they make a feature story out of it. Newspapers raved about Eastham's service station on Wisconsin Avenue in Bethesda, Maryland. Two Eastham attendants *run* toward every car that pulls up to the pumps. "Good morning!" they yell out to the driver. They scurry about swiftly pumping gas, cleaning every inch of glass, and shouting for the driver to unlatch the car's hood. Hands fly among the hoses and belts, checking oil and water levels.

A drop of sweat falls from one employee's forehead and lands on the front bumper. Quickly he bends over and wipes it off with a clean cloth.

Can you believe it?

The entire service process lasts about three minutes.

Bad service is seen by many consumers as a *personal insult.* They become angry, depressed, or insecure when salespeople ignore them, snap at them or hurry to get rid of them. They are offended when salespeople haven't considered their customers important enough for them to learn the answers to common questions about the merchandise or service they sell.

Kroger Food Stores surveyed consumers and found that more than half expected that they would be mistreated in some way. They expected to be ignored, to wait in long lines and to have clerks say "I don't know" and "Sorry, I'm going on break."

How many consumers have experienced service so bad that they felt like complaining about it?

Nearly all of them, I believe.

No government agency maintains a Helpfulness Index, however, so statistics on service level don't exist. We are left to the opinions of experts. And experts in customer service say that service in our service society generally stinks.

Jason had been saving his money for more than a year to buy an expensive home entertainment center. He went to the store on a Tuesday afternoon, deliberately arriving after the lunch-hour rush, at a time when he thought business probably would be slow.

He planned to look at the various systems, listen to how they sounded, and then ask a salesperson to explain features of the various systems that he found most desirable in his price range.

There were two salesclerks on the floor when Jason arrived and, as he hoped, they were not busy. One approached him eagerly, saying, "Can I help you, sir?"

"Not right now," said Jason. "I just want to look around for a while."

The clerk's smile froze. He said nothing, then walked back to the other clerk. Although the salesperson lowered his voice, Jason heard him derisively say, "Looker. Guess it's going to be another bad week for my paycheck."

Then the two clerks proceeded to talk to each other about a movie they had seen. When Jason was ready to ask questions, the clerk dismissed him with a wave of the hand saying, "The signs say what you get. We can't go taking out the spec sheets unless you know which one you want to buy."

Jason was as disappointed as he was angry.

He left, knowing he would have to try again somewhere else on another day.

"Another slow week," the salesman said, never realizing how close he came to making a $1,000 sale.

Mary was in the market for a new car when she went to the showroom of a local dealership. She knew the features she wanted and the general price range she could afford. But when she arrived a football game was on the widescreen television in the waiting area set aside for customers having their cars serviced. The salespeople were gathered around the set, sipping coffee and cheering the home team on.

Mary understood the loyalty. She was a fan herself and had hoped to watch the game. But this was the only time she had to get the car and she hoped that she could make her purchase and leave quickly. She had no questions to ask. Yet when she tried to get someone to wait on her, the sales staff kept saying, "Just a minute, lady."

What they didn't anticipate was that Mary's patience lasted only *five* minutes.

It was another three weeks before she could take time again to look for a new car — at a different dealership.

TALK ABOUT BAD SERVICE

Bad service takes many forms. How many of these characters and situations do you recognize?

1. High school students working at minimum wage in a local hardware store who are so uninformed about products that any question other than "How much does it cost?" is met with a blank stare.

2. Home electronics or computer salespeople, or auto parts store employees who are condescending toward you because you ask questions about a product's features and applications. They toss off incomplete or unbelievable answers to your questions like they would throw scraps to a dog.

3. Banks with long lines and teller windows that close just when it's your turn.

4. Doctors who are always "running late." Their office secretaries make appointments for specific times, but you haven't seen the doctor at that time in ten years. Doctors apparently overschedule to maximize their incomes: Some patients might not keep their appointments, you see.

5. Salespeople who obviously feel that playing the customer-is-always-right role is degrading. They give crisp, cold, and abrupt service, rarely establishing eye contact with you. They usually glance at you, just barely avoiding rudeness, because they realize that they must be helpful and friendly since that's their job. But, for sure, they're not going to do any more than they must do to keep you from complaining to the manager. Service is not something they give with great enthusiasm.

6. In a department store, boutique, appliance store, or government office, employees walk by you as if you're a mannequin. Or, if they can't avoid responding to you, they speak while continuing to fill in records or to stock shelves.

7. Restaurants that overbook or understaff, thereby "encouraging" you to wait in the bar for your table and to buy expensive drinks.

   Money magazine observed that some restaurants have come to be noted for their "hors deals" rather than their "hors d'oeuvres." The service situation in restaurants, says Money, reflects the rise in dining out and the decline of common courtesy.

A restaurant in West Los Angeles is notorious for overbookings that result in waits of up to an hour.

A New York City restaurant that caters to employees on Publishing Row and to the arts crowd also is well known for bad service. One man and his guest were shown into a tiny waiting alcove when they showed up for a reservation that had been confirmed and then reconfirmed. An hour later they were given a table, with no apology for the long wait.

Sometimes diners dine longer than a restaurant expects; but, the maitre d' could have shown some concern; and he could have apologized.

The late comedian Freddie Prinze chose the problem of indifference as a comedic trademark. No matter how simple a request — from "Do you have the time?" to "Please pass the salt" — he always said: "It's not my job."

"Have you ever tried to buy something in a fashionable shop if you are a female, gray-haired, over-50, and a bit flabby?" asks Barbara S. Bach of Indianapolis. "Don't bother. Salesclerks will avoid you as if you have the plague. Next to the unaccompanied child sent out to buy something at the last minute for a harried parent, over-50, fat, and faded females are the most ignored customers in the world."

She couldn't get anyone to wait on her so she finally picked up the skirt and headed for the door. Three security people converged on her.

"However," she said, "they didn't offer to wait on me."

She urged "over-50, overweight, and overlooked" females to buy from mail-order catalogs.

This is *not* the way things ought to be in a civilized society. As a service to people who are indecisive and hesitant about complaining, here are valid grounds for complaint:

- UNWILLINGNESS TO ANSWER QUESTIONS; IGNORANCE OF MERCHANDISE: Some salespeople give flippant, partial answers to questions like scraps to a dog, while continuing to fill out forms, stock shelves, or talk with a friend.

- AVOIDING; IGNORING: Employees seem to be on perpetual coffee break. They disappear as you approach. Sometimes they walk by you without even looking at you. You find them absorbed in personal conversations, chatting on the phone, or too busy shelf-stocking to be bothered by a mere customer.

- COLD, IMPERSONAL MANNER: Service is crisp and abrupt, not one whit better than necessary to avoid the ire of supervisors. Service employees give the appearance of helpfulness. Some hospitals and doctors treat patients like cadavers, working on them, talking over them...never speaking to them.

- FAST, CARELESS SERVICE: To some service employees you are an unwelcome interruption. They want to finish with you quickly so they can get on with more "important" business like discussing last night's date. Sometimes they ignore you, thinking that shunning will encourage you to leave. One veteran female consumer says: "I never leave. I interrupt them until I get their attention."

- THE BRUSH-OFF: You're treated like a football, handed off and passed all over the field. After you've become tired of feeling like a pigskin, you give up, vowing revenge. Some government employees seem to be very good at giving the brush-off.

- ❑ PROMISES NOT KEPT: Attorneys say: "It's in the mail." Furniture stores schedule a delivery date, then ignore it without telling you. Appliance repair technicians promise to come on Tuesday, but they don't show up and don't call. Moving companies promise an arrival date for your belongings and miss it by days, and you set up housekeeping in a motel.
- ❑ FAILURE TO RETURN PHONE CALLS: You call and leave messages repeatedly. Your calls aren't returned because you are a problem that the business does not wish to solve.

You deserve better.

Chapter 2

FIGHTING BACK PAYS OFF

"Fight back!
You don't have to take it!"

"When products proved poorly made, items arrived broken or food spoiled, I used to throw them away, convinced that to complain would only draw form letters...(But now) I use the telephone and the typewriter. I get results."

— DAWN SOVA
Women's Day Magazine

Two windows fell out of her Ford, so Gayle Knutson of St. Louis Park, Minnesota, wrote to the Ford Motor Company about it. By return mail she received a certificate authorizing her to have the windows repaired. The cost of the window work and other repairs was about $500, paid by Ford.

Terry Rikolta, 43, of Bloomfield Hills, Michigan, mother of four, objected to the way female characters were treated in a certain TV situation comedy. She wrote letters to all 45 sponsors of the show. At last report none of them had withdrawn sponsorship; but still Ms. Rikolta got results. She appeared on the network TV shows "Nightline," "CBS This Morning," and "Entertainment Tonight" — campaigning for her position.

Joe Cimmet, freelance artist, and his wife, Eve, find that most businesses settle complaints graciously. One night they went to their local theater, expecting a relaxing evening. Instead, they spent the night straining to hear a scratchy, poorly amplified sound track. They decided that they would confront the manager.

What happened? He gave them free movie tickets.

Dawn Sova wrote in *Woman's Day* magazine: "When products proved poorly made, items arrived broken or food spoiled, I used to throw them away, convinced that to complain would only draw form letters...(But now) I use the telephone and the typewriter. I get results."

But, still, far more people complain among themselves than complain to an offending business. A major national survey found, in fact, that only 10 percent of people disgusted with service actually complain.

Why? Some people are too polite to complain. Or, they think that only yahoos complain.

Others simply don't have the self-esteem or personality type to confront others, even when they are certain that their complaints are justified.

COMPLAIN EVERY TIME

If the inclination to shut up instead of to speak up is ever going to change, consumers must undergo an attitude change. They must make complaining the rule instead of the exception.

Look at it this way: It's logical to complain in our society. Consumers wield great influence here. If large numbers of consumers consistently press their displeasure upon business, then more businesses will realize that good service is in their best interests and will provide it.

Fight back! You don't have to *take it.*

There is benefit to the spirit in fighting back.

There's pleasure and satisfaction in winning fair treatment.

You ought to complain because it's *right* to do so — because businesses are *wrong* to make you wait for 20 minutes...*wrong* to turn loose salespeople who know little more about the merchandise they're selling than how to turn it on and off.

Since you pay for service, you're being cheated when you get neglect and even insults. So, complain to avoid injustice... and also headaches, high blood pressure, and hyperventilation.

When an employee treats you as if you have B.O., *fight back* for the sake of all other consumers...and for the sake of the majority of businesses that will almost always jump through a hoop to satisfy their customers...as soon as they *know* that the customer is *dis*satisfied.

FIGHTING BACK IS IN STYLE

More people *are* fighting back. Fighting back may be a sign of the times. There's an upsurge in personal action throughout our society. People believe more than ever that they can change government, social and economic conditions, and the way business is conducted. And they're *doing it*.

So, confront businesspeople who continually ignore you. Don't allow them to intimidate you into silence when you know very well that even by business's own standards you are being poorly served.

Fight back! *Demand* service. Don't let a single example of rudeness or socializing at your expense go unreported.

One of your obstacles in your fight-back crusade will be managers and executives who believe that customers deserve only merchandise — or service that they specifically pay for.

Any pre-sale or post-sale service is a bonus that customers have no right to *expect* and are unjustified in criticizing, the businesspeople believe.

These are likely to be the same businesspeople who say "Caveat emptor!" ("Let the buyer beware."), as if it is the ultimate rationale for bad service.

Well...fine. If they want to throw down the gauntlet, let's pick it up. "Caveat emptor!" We *will* beware. And when we beware, business better beware, too.

We aren't going to hand over our money without insisting that we get full product or service value. "Full value" means "full service."

We will consider a transaction *incomplete* until we are satisfied.

CHAPTER 3

SHOULD YOU COMPLAIN?

"Complaints are opportunities to rectify customers' problems."

— THE OFFICE OF CONSUMER AFFAIRS

You should complain.

Complain to organizations whose poor service is part of their lean-and-mean management plan that reduces the number of employees who make person-to-person contact with consumers.

Leveraged buyouts and hostile takeovers never are consummated for the purpose of *improving* service.

According to the National Planning Assn., a Washington-based business research organization, corporate downsizing and plant closings have displaced (de-employed) more than two million workers every year since the late 1970s.

If you read the newspapers you've seen it happen many times: Multinational corporations seeking even more profit take over companies whose assets they covet. They spend millions on the financial transaction itself, but not a cent to maintain or to develop courteous, helpful service.

A few months later poor service reaps its reward: A public outcry in the press, a demonstration outside corporate headquarters, or government pressure forces a company to hire a vice president of customer service, to announce a new customer service program...or even to provide better service.

The way that poor service develops, sometimes, is through the "demotivation" of employees. After a merger or takeover their fear of being fired distracts them from their work. They become disillusioned, dispirited, and unmotivated. Service declines.

As a result of mergers and unwillingness of companies to spend money to develop quality service, people keep coming up with new horror stories to tell their friends, who have their own stories to tell.

DON'T BE EMBARRASSED

There's no need to be *embarrassed* about complaining. You aren't hurting an organization by complaining. Quite the contrary: You're helping. Why? Because you're bringing a problem to the attention of management, a service that will be appreciated by most executives, unless you swear at them while you're describing the problem.

The best organizations know that it is in their interests for customers who are dissatisfied to complain. That's because when customers complain, then businesses can correct. If customers don't complain, businesses cannot correct.

So, don't bite your lip and let the bile rise, or clamp your mouth shut and let the pressure build up. Prevent a heart attack by letting management know, immediately, about bad service.

Here's a concise list of the benefits of good customer service for business, the sort of list that the president of the International Customer Service Association would read from the podium at the group's annual meeting:

"Satisfied customers return. A solid base of satisfied, loyal customers minimizes the cost of attracting new customers. That cost is five times higher than the cost of *keeping* existing customers, calculated by a standard generally accepted by customer service pros."

NO EXCUSES SERVICE

Most retailers operate on profit margins of about 1-to-3 percent. Add to meager profit the apparent mass flight of competent salespeople, and it's a wonder that retailing survives.

This said, there's still no excuse for shabby treatment at the hands of rude salespeople, or for roadblocks thrown in your path when you try to get replacement or repair service for a new product that doesn't work, or for appliances or furniture with six-week-guaranteed delivery that are still "on the way" after two months.

Good service prevents the need for a company to spend money to attract new customers and clients to replace those that bad service has alienated.

So, when customers complain and goad organizations into service improvements, they are helping them save money.

When customers complain they are more likely to continue buying from the organization they complain to, even if they don't receive total satisfaction. This may seem strange, but it's true. The Office of Consumer Affairs states: "Although many managers view complaints as a drain on resources...complaints may be an extremely valuable marketing asset...Complaints are opportunities to rectify customers' problems.

"Companies that respond to these 'opportunities' are rewarded through continuing brand loyalty, generally in direct proportion to the degree of their responsiveness."

Nordstrom Inc., the highly regarded, Seattle-based apparel, shoes, and soft goods retailer that's been in business since 1901, has proved that retailers can do very well, indeed, when they listen to customer complaints and when they work hard at reducing the number of reasons for complaining. The company enjoyed the highest sales per square foot of any department store in the country, $310, before the recession that began in 1991. That was $160 more than the average.

Nordstrom has stores in more than 40 cities in the Pacific Northwest, California, Minneapolis, and eastern cities.

In its National Consumer Survey the U.S. Office of Consumer Affairs found a strong relationship between complaining and *brand loyalty*. When minor complaints were resolved to the consumer's satisfaction, 70 percent of complainants reported that they would keep on buying.

Among those whose minor complaints were not satisfactorily resolved, 46 percent still indicated that they would repurchase the problem product or service.

But, the same National Consumer Survey found that only about a third of customers with minor problems who didn't complain at all said they would repurchase.

So, you see, complaining is good for business.

Feel good about complaining.

Consumers have always known that good service yields competitive advantage.

Any business can train and motivate their employees to provide friendly, competent service...if they want to. There's simply no excuse for surly, uninformed service.

Indeed, good service can be achieved with just a simple change in attitude by front-line service people led by managers and executives — plus changes in procedure that expedite service.

Here's an example of a problem that could be solved more easily if business would simply change a procedure — staffing level, in this case: You're on the phone listening to a repetitious message that says, "All service representatives are busy." Every once in a while a recorded voice says, "Thank you for being patient."

But, you *aren't* patient. Hearing a voice expressing the assumption that you are patient when you aren't is like being thanked for your vote by a politician you voted against.

After the seventh or eighth "Thank you for being patient," you feel like blowing a high-pitched whistle into the phone receiver even if you know that the voice you hear is recorded.

In many cases, preventing this aggravation would require only scheduling the same staff for more hours during peak calling periods so that real people could answer the phones promptly.

Some business, government, and non-profit organizations provide outstanding customer service. But, many others treat customers and clients as if they are obstacles or inconveniences instead of the source of their survival.

It's up to customers and clients to help these organizations see the light. If you hesitate to complain, remember that organizations that treat customers as 'adversaries' instead of as friends are beneficiaries of your complaints, not victims of them.

Chapter 4

WE DON'T COMPLAIN ENOUGH

"I'm mad as hell...and I'm not going to take it anymore!"

From the Movie
NETWORK

"It's no wonder that in the marketplace or in the halls of government those who are organized and knowledgeable [get] their way. And those people who abdicate, delegate, or vegetate are taken."

—INTRODUCTION TO *A Public Citizen's Action Manual*

Some consumers spend thousands of hours driving a new automobile, eating food from a supermarket, or shopping for clothing, but not one minute to correct overpricing, fraud, and hazards associated with these products!

Service is bad largely because consumers allow business, government units, and private organizations to get by with it.

They just walk away, shaking their heads, "telling off" the salesperson in their imaginations, and visualizing themselves relating their experience to their long-suffering spouses or friends.

Shoppers are sheep!

Consumers feel that:

1. Complaining isn't worth their time and effort.
2. It won't do any good.
3. They don't know how or where to complain.
4. They might be embarrassed if they complain.

We do not complain enough even though most of us experience bad service regularly.

A Hackensack, New Jersey, newspaper told a story about a woman who waited at an untended cash register for a full 10 minutes. Finally, she yelled loudly enough to turn a few heads: "Will *somebody* please take my money?"

Another woman tells of an experience in Bamberger's department store. She was the *only* customer in the Lady's Dresses department. Bored salespeople stood around in clusters. Yet, no salesperson broke away from a group to take her payment, even though it was obvious that the woman had finished her shopping and was looking for someone to help her.

Finally, she approached a group of salespeople talking animatedly. She asked for assistance. One of the salespeople, a woman, said: "Just a minute, honey." And she went back to exchanging child-rearing anecdotes with two other women. The customer complained to the department manager. She also cancelled her charge account.

Gary Shade of Apple Valley, Minnesota, got mad at a pizza parlor. His family ordered a pizza at 6:25 p.m. and they were told that it would be ready at 7:00. But, it wasn't ready until 7:40. Even then a clerk told the family that they'd have to wait another 10 minutes while she made the garlic bread.

That's when Shade asked to see the manager.

"Although six other people waited as long or longer than we did, no one complained to the cashier or to the manager," said Shade. "Not one person."

This extreme tolerance for bad service can be explained by the fact that some consumers have received bad service for so long that they *expect* it; so, they don't even bother to complain anymore. If they did, the picture would look even worse for business, for government, and for private organizations.

Here's one more incident that indicates that consumers don't complain often enough: Every time Bette Schwartzberg shopped at a certain A&P store on the East Coast, which she did as seldom as possible, she vowed, "Never again."

"I simply could not get out of that store without being aggravated, whether it was because only one checkout register was open with a long line in front of it...or something else," she said. "I can remember several times wanting only a few things and deciding to just leave and buy them at a convenience store even though they cost more there."

In a neighborhood Grand Union store, says Ms. Schwartzberg, "I am invariably impressed. The manager himself opens a new cash register whenever lines get more than three people long."

Ms. Schwartzberg's experiences demonstrate that businesses *can* provide good service if they want to and that it is every customer's duty to make them want to.

THE FACTS: PEOPLE DON'T COMPLAIN

A study found that only one out of 26 customers who are dissatisfied actually complain. And only a fraction of the complainers pursue a solution to their problem beyond the seller — to the manufacturer...or to government agencies and consumer groups.

An oft-cited survey of consumers with service problems found that more than 70 percent of consumers fully *justified* in complaining don't do so.

Perhaps more people would express their dissatisfaction if they knew that 56 percent of all complaints result in satisfaction for the complainer, according to one study.

Still another study determined that a fourth of the average business's customers are willing to switch to competitors. That ought to strike fear into the hearts of businesspeople.

However, many dissatisfied customers never get around to "voting with their feet." Says James Donnelly Jr., author of *Close to the Customer*: "I've had people tell me that they hate their bank, but they haven't left yet. Or, they hate a certain airline, but they continue to fly it."

If switching your business is intolerably inconvenient, then apply the strategies described in this book.

Switching your business to a competitor remains one of the best recourses for consumers.

But, businesses who give bad service *know* that most dissatisfied customers don't complain. The deafening silence from their customers gives them permission to continue the same poor service policy. When you think about it, what motivation does a business with uncomplaining customers have to provide service?

It's up to *you* to motivate these companies.

Service becomes even less important to these businesses the day that they realize that customers that switch to competitors are replaced by competitors' customers switching to *them*.

Poor service wastes your time. That's intolerable when two- income families are common. Both wage-earners fight the clock. Husbands and wives are so rushed to get home to do their family chores that organizations that waste their time win their enmity.

So, it's not surprising that people feel that complaining is too expensive and time-consuming. This was proved by a survey of 2400 randomly chosen households. The survey was reported in the book *When Consumers Complain*, by Dr. Arthur Best of the New York Law School.

Other studies find low rates of satisfaction with the results of complaining. A National Consumer Survey reported more than 40 percent of households experiencing consumer problems were unhappy with action that business took to resolve their complaints.

So they stop complaining.

EMBARRASSMENT

Consumers don't want other shoppers or service employees to look at them with disdain. They don't want to be called whiners or jerks for complaining...even if an incompetent employee was guilty of being rude and lazy.

Bad-service employees have this embarrassment shtick down pat. Just *try* to get away without tipping a cab driver and he'll teach you true embarrassment, quickly.

If you leave a small tip, a waitperson might follow you to the door with it — even into the street — and throw the money at you, proclaiming in a loud voice: "Here, you need this more than I do!"

In the mind of many service workers, a tip is due for *any* service, whether it is friendly and willing or surly and reluctant.

CONSUMERS EXPECT BAD SERVICE

One consumer authority says: "In some industries people have gotten mediocre service for so long that they take it for granted. Take the New York subway system. People are so happy to survive the trip that dirty cars are not important."

A major retail food chain surveyed consumers, in focus groups, and found that *more than half* expected that service would be bad and that they would be mistreated.

They expected to be ignored and to wait in long lines. They expected to have checkout people say, "Sorry, I'm going on break."

People who expect bad service are rarely surprised when the anticipated bad service occurs. Nor are they likely to do anything about it.

IS POOR SERVICE YOUR OWN FAULT?

Gary Shade, the astute consumer from Apple Valley, Minnesota, who complained about slow pizza delivery, said: "It amazes me that as Americans we can sit back and truly believe that the current trade imbalance is not our fault, that it is the fault of the Japanese or our own government, when we accept service like this.

"The more I experience poor service the more I believe that it is our fault. It's our fault when we don't raise our voices when confronted with exceptionally poor service or quality. Have we become so accustomed or conditioned to bad service that we accept it without challenge?

"How is a company to know, without consumer feedback, that they must change?" Shade concluded.

With the proper attitude, you can get good service almost every time you buy anything. Say to yourself: "I am going to *demand* good service."

So, *ask* for the service that you expect. Use phrases such as "Would you mind...?" Or: "Will you please...?" Complete these phrases with words that describe the service you require.

You'll get what you ask for, almost every time, unless you ask for something unreasonable. But, you will *know* when you are being unreasonable; so you won't really expect to get what you ask for.

If a miracle occurred and every consumer complained *every time* they didn't get what was ordered...or had to wait half an hour for somebody to acknowledge their existence...or had to argue through lunch hour to get a service employee to acknowledge an obvious billing error ...or needed a blood hound just to *find* a service worker ...if every one of these people would complain *every time*, then the bad businesses, the inconsiderate government, and the sleepy private organizations would "get the message" overnight.

Go ahead, America. Just like in the movie *Network*, lean out your windows and yell: "I'm mad as hell...and I'm not going to take it anymore!"

CHAPTER 5

COMPLAINING PROTOCOL: USE OIL INSTEAD OF VINEGAR

"Be sure you are right, then go ahead."

— DAVY CROCKETT, AMERICAN FRONTIERSMAN

If you are *right*, you have Abraham Lincoln behind you. He said in his Second Inaugural Address: "Let us have faith that right makes might, and in that faith let us to the end dare to do our duty as we understand it."

Now, what better guidance could a consumer complainer want?

(What, you don't believe that Crockett and Lincoln were referring to complaining about bad service?)

We interpret Lincoln and Crockett to mean, in modern terms: Make sure that you have a valid case and that it is not *you* who is at fault.

Maintain a calm and reasoned frame of mind by reminding yourself periodically that there are at least as many alert and helpful, friendly, and knowledgeable service workers as there are indolent, insulting, and insouciant service workers. The problem is that the bad ones are so *very* noticeable that they block our view of their friendly, helpful, knowledgeable, and professional co-workers.

But, *try* to notice the good service. If you don't accentuate the positive, you'll criticize unfairly. You will judge harshly and unreasonably, thereby dampening the desire of even the competent service employees and their supervisors to answer your requests and solve your problems. You will...shall we say..."lose credibility."

Answer for yourself the question: Just how accommodating do you expect business to be?

This accommodating? A sign, relating to irate, complaining consumer showed a store manager talking to a complainer: "Would it satisfy you if we would refund your money, replace your purchase, go out of business, and shoot the manager?"

Or *this* accommodating? "If we don't get you your pizza in five minutes we'll make your car payment." (Radio commercial for Gung Ho Stir Fry, a chain of restaurants.)

Don't let your face droop into an expectant scowl whenever you enter a store. Don't let anticipation of bad service cloud your judgment.

Be constructive. One of your functions should be (shouldn't it?) to encourage good service so that you will see more of it. Do this by complimenting good service people... *and* by calling bad service to the attention of perpetrators. Inform their superiors and the president of the company or even public or private watchdog groups when bad service is very gratuitous and insulting.

Here are some guidelines that a level-headed person who wants to avoid burning his/her bridges behind them might want to follow in complaining, negotiating, appealing, or constructively criticizing:

1. BE REASONABLE. If you really want satisfaction and you aren't just letting off steam, it's important to avoid being critical. Criticism puts people on the defensive. If you appear to be reasonable, people find it harder to tune you out. Skillful complainers agree: An effective tactic is to present yourself as a reasonable person who needs help.

2. COMPLIMENT. Pat Bear, who runs an information retrieval firm in New York City, starts her complaints with a compliment. She reports: "I went to the buyer at Saks Fifth Avenue and said: 'Everything I ever bought from Saks has been terrific. I was surprised when this happened.'" (The seams in her boots tore open. Saks exchanged them.)

3. AVOID ANGER. Spiteful letters and hand-waving harangues in person are counterproductive. Just present the facts, soberly, clearly, forcefully. Anger and sarcasm merely put your opponent on the defensive. Besides, strongly negative emotions tend to give you a headache. If you are angry, people focus on your anger instead of on your problem. Sarcasm and excessive cleverness also detract from your message. So, appeal, at first. Don't demand.

4. AVOID DRAMATIC DISPLAYS. Don't try to get your way by creating a disturbance. In a hotel, don't threaten the room clerk with: "Since you won't honor my room reservation I'll just sack out in your lobby. First, I'll put on my pajamas. Then, I'll... "

> Parking your car in front of the dealership from which you bought it and mounting a sign that says "I bought this lemon from Smith Auto Co." definitely will harden the negotiating position of Smith Auto Co.
>
> Just lock eyes with the person in authority who receives your complaint and speak in a firm, steady but reasonable voice in presenting your case. There's always time to get hard-nosed after you've tried the soft sell.

When you're in a restaurant, don't get mad and demand to see the manager after five minutes of waiting because you had a bad day. Don't become prematurely indignant. Save your indignation for times when it is really justified.

Don't use a waitress or a salesclerk as a convenient whipping post, as an escape valve for the anger you feel because you had an argument with your boss. Or because you're having marriage problems or your boyfriend or girlfriend left you. Or because your team lost a game.

When you complain, be firm but be pleasant. Rage just makes it easy for a business to dismiss you as a crank. Speak firmly but calmly. Don't threaten or attack a serviceperson orally. Stick to poor-service issues.

A calm approach almost always is effective. Unfortunately, many people lapse into a tirade the moment they open their mouths to complain. That's because they're afraid. Or they're uneasy. Their loud, threatening manner is false bravado.

"Many people gripe just to get something off their chests," says the national manager of Autocap, a trade group that handles thousands of complaints from disgruntled car owners every year.

To be very sure that you are reasonable and blameless, recite the facts of your experience to a good friend or family member. If they, too, think that you were "done wrong," then, by all means, proceed with your complaint.

Some customer service professionals find that the very word "complain" is counterproductive. Herb Nierenberg uses the word "negotiate." He wrote the book *The Art of Negotiating.* Stephen Pollan, who wrote *Getting People to Say Yes*, believes there's value in "appeal" instead of "complain."

You might like the term "constructive criticism."

No matter what words you use, fix in your mind the inadvertent nature of most poor service.

Dr. Edward D. Joseph, psychiatrist at Mt. Sinai Medical Center, New York, said, in referring to poor service: "It's important to remember that most 'injuries' are inflicted impersonally (and) without malice."

CHAPTER 6

PREPARATION: JUST IN CASE

"Anyone can gather facts and figures and present them in a clear and logical way."

If you want to stop being apologetic and fearful to service and manufacturing businesses that make it corporate policy to intimidate or to confuse you, then keep all your sales slips. Keep cash register receipts, credit card receipts, cancelled checks, product tags, labels or warranties, care information sheets, repair orders, copies of letters that you send to the company or store, and even keep company advertising. Keep any piece of paper that comes with a purchase

Under law, customers must be informed of the name and address of every manufacturer of food, drug, and cosmetic products when they purchase them. Many other products have this information, too. So, one thing you accomplish by saving the paper that accompanies a purchase is that you have the information you would need to write a letter to the manufacturer, if doing so becomes necessary.

If your experiences with rotten service have made a fanatic out of you, you could expand your income tax record-keeping system to routinely include notes about your reactions to treatment you receive, to quality of products purchased.

GET THE FACTS

Besides accurate and complete information about your buying experiences, also obtain names and titles of people you meet while purchasing, so you can address any letters or make phone calls to individuals *by name.*

The easiest place to find phone numbers and locations of the businesses you deal with at a retail level is in the telephone directory. Company headquarters, regional offices, local distribution centers, and sales offices that can be found in phone books often will handle your problem locally — or refer you to the proper individual and location in the company.

Zip Codes for the addresses you find in phone directories, by the way, are included in a Zip Code section in most phone books.

When you make that first phone call to a business whose service you are dissatisfied with, have pen and paper handy so you can jot down names and titles of people you speak with as well as phone numbers and dates of calls.

Mike Berger, a computer journalist, prepared. He was hit with an exorbitant phone bill for calls billed to his home phone number. The trouble was that he didn't make the calls. He lives alone and he was traveling during the time the calls were made.

The phone company wouldn't accept his claim that he didn't make the calls. So, he contacted the state Public Utilities Commission, presented his case, and asked for a public hearing. The PUC obliged.

Berger went home and threw himself into preparations for the hearing. He analyzed his bills for a year, using his computer. Then he prepared computer-generated graphs to illustrate that the expensive phone calls he was billed for were a deviation from his normal calling pattern as shown by the graphs.

Berger convinced the PUC that he didn't make the calls. So, the regulatory body instructed the phone company to delete the cost of the calls from his billing.

Not many people can use a computer to coerce business into fairness, but anyone can gather facts and figures and present them in a clear and logical way.

Success will be much easier when you keep all the paper that you receive when you make a purchase.

CHAPTER 7

THE WORKING DOCUMENT

"A working document is a statement of all the facts, names and arguments pertaining to your situation."

"You are a person to be recokoned with."

One fine form of preparation for a by-phone or in-person meeting with a company representative is a "working document."

A working document is a *statement* of all the facts, names, and arguments (appeals) pertaining to your situation. This will be your guide when you make phone calls and write letters.

The document should contain date, time, and topics of phone calls and later visits to the store or office and names of contacts. Of course, it should also contain a careful description of circumstances surrounding the event that caused your complaint.

If you can type the document, fine. A typed document implies competency and often wins faster company response if for no other reason than that it's easier to read than a hand-written communication. Companies will conclude that you are a person to be reckoned with.

A hand-written document still is likely to receive fair, if slower, treatment. Companies want to hear about customer dissatisfaction so they can prevent future dissatisfaction.

With your working document and with the papers you've saved, you're ready to begin a complaint process.

CHAPTER 8

HOW TO COMPLAIN EFFECTIVELY: STRATEGIES

Ten Guidelines for Effective Complaining:

1. Have your facts straight.
2. Be clear about what you want.
3. Write to the president if other calls fail.
4. Never talk to anyone who doesn't have the authority to do what you want.
5. Escalate your complaint quickly.
6. Speak firmly.
7. State that you are unwilling to let the matter be prolonged.
8. Set a reasonable time limit for action.
9. Conclude phone calls with a restatement of any agreement that you reach.
10. Keep clear copies of every letter you send.

Let's say that you receive rude or incompetent service from a front-line serviceperson. Since that employee is part of the problem, you are unlikely to receive complete satisfaction from that employee.

Attempt to get your complaint satisfied by the offending employee by making a direct request to the employee for satisfaction. A service employee is not very likely to say "No" to a direct request. Why? Because employees know that their bosses would disapprove.

As a consumer, you know by experience or by instinct that when you go to the boss after the employee has given you the cold shoulder, the boss often will lean heavily in your direction.

If the employee refuses your request and refuses to provide *normal service*, you have an effective weapon to use against them — their own behavior. You can use that behavior as a lever to pry good service out of a store, government office, or other organization.

Sometimes the boss will say "No," too. But, usually this will happen only when *you* are clearly wrong — or clearly rude. Maybe it's clear, too, that you were just looking for a way to express your anger about the speeding ticket you got on your way to the store.

If nobody listens to you, continue complaining until you reach the president of the company... if you're really determined to solve your problem.

When you complain to a president, convince him or her that you are only the first complainer in a long line of dissatisfied customers. Point out that salesclerks who handled your purchase badly most likely are treating other customers the same way. If this kind of treatment continues, you can say, the business will be in danger, no matter how well established it is now.

But, if a manager or supervisor succeeds in persuading the president that your complaint is not worth responding to, then go on to these organizations, in sequence:

1. The industry's self-regulatory body, such as the Furniture Industry Consumer Action Panel (FICAP) or the Major Appliance Consumer Action Panel (MACAP). They have fine reputations for service. MACAP, for instance, cut through red tape and found a consumer's missing living room suite in a large store's warehouse. It was delivered within three days, after the consumer had waited a month before contacting MACAP.

2. Consumer organizations such as those listed in Directory of State and Local Consumer Groups, available in most libraries. Or, contact the Better Business Bureau or a local or state consumer protection agency. (State consumer protection offices often are located in the attorney general's department.)

3. A federal government agency, such as the Food and Drug Administration or the Federal Trade Commission.

Finally, try arbitration, Small Claims court, or even a law suit, if you are clearly in the right and if a company has repeatedly refused you.

In some circumstances, you will get perfectly good results by going to a customer service department in person or by calling a company's customer service "800" number. You are a good judge of situations that ought to be brought to the attention of an organization's customer service department.

Customer service employees either can handle your problem directly — they are being given greater responsibility for satisfying your request — or they know how to bring your case to the attention of top management.

If you suspect that you are being given the brush, bounced from person to person, like a ball off a bumper in a pin ball machine, call a halt with a threat to continue accosting the company until they respond appropriately.

One woman began to occupy so much of the time available on a mail-order clothing company's fax machine that a manager ordered the customer service department to solve her problem immediately.

Always make sure that the person you see has the *authority* to make a decision, though. If he or she doesn't, find somebody who does.

You might strike out in trying to resolve a service problem by dealing with someone at the location where you received poor service. Or, perhaps you're too reserved to confront employees face-to-face. So, go home and launch your campaign there.

It isn't fair to assume that you *will* be rebuffed at the purchase location, however. Most complaints are resolved long before they reach top executives such as store managers, company vice presidents, or the president. Business should be given credit for this.

But... the few complaints that must be carried to the top because you couldn't get favorable response from first-contact employees are precisely the complaints that cause most high blood pressure and gastro-intestinal upsets among consumers.

GET THE FACTS

Make sure that you have accurate and complete information before you initiate a complaint. You might even be so annoyed that you carry a microcassette recorder in the top pocket of your blouse or shirt and record a repetition of the same awful service, if you need more details. Just nonchalantly reach inside your pocket and press the *record* button.

These modern, supersensitive micro-recorders pick up voices clearly about 10 feet away in a relatively noisy environment.

When an employee says something like, "Sorry, it's company policy" and they suggest, in effect, that you get lost, then you'll have the goods on them.

Play back the recording for the customer service rep.

To encourage good service, transcribe any recordings of cheery, helpful responses by salespeople. (You're a good citizen.) Send the transcription to the place of business with a note saying when and where the good service occurred.

The exceptional serviceperson will hear about it and benefit from the recognition.

You will need to obtain names and titles in preparation for calling or writing anyone.

Find phone numbers in local phone directories or dial the information number (Area Code + 555-1212) for the city in which the company facility you are trying to reach is located. If people that you reach at these numbers can't handle your problem, they'll usually refer you to someone who can.

Many companies have set up toll-free "800" numbers. Often this hot line number is listed on packages or labels.

Call the telephone company's toll-free information number (1-800-555-1212) to find out if the company you wish to call has an "800" number.

Employees working these hot lines are trained to know policy and procedure and to tell you what to do and whom to contact.

One way to determine where a company is located is to look at the product tags or labels or on warranties or printed product information and care information sheets that accompany merchandise.

But, if you've lost all sources of a manufacturer's name or phone number, try the Better Business Bureau. The BBB lists many manufacturers, but not all of them. Other sources of this information are *Standard and Poor's Register* and *Consumers' Index to Product Evaluations and Information Sources*.

Most libraries carry one or both of these reference books. *Standard and Poor's* lists the names of company presidents and other corporate officers, too.

Final resources for information that you need to contact retail or manufacturing companies are two membership groups for customer service professionals:

SOCIETY OF CONSUMER AFFAIRS
PROFESSIONALS IN BUSINESS (SOCAP)
801 North Fairfax Street, 4th Floor
Alexandria, VA 22314
703-519-3700

INTERNATIONAL CUSTOMER SERVICE ASSN. (ICSA)
401 North Michigan Avenue
Chicago, IL 60611
312-321-6800

It's effective strategy to speak firmly but calmly instead of screaming and waving your arms when you complain. Don't threaten.

Be persistent. Persistence is the ace up your sleeve, one of the basic rules for successful complaining. Businesspeople, you see, find it difficult to rebuff a persistent customer. They're hampered by a voice in their minds saying: "It's bad business to say 'No' to a customer."

GUIDELINES

Here are "Ten Guidelines for Effective Complaining":

1. Have your facts straight. Refer to dates, names, and specific incidents. Support your statements with documentation, whenever documents are available.
2. Be clear about what you want. Demand a specific remedy. This is more effective than going into an aimless tirade.
3. Write to the president of the company, if repeated phone calls to a supervisor or the customer service department fail.
4. Never talk (or write) to anyone who doesn't have the authority to do what you want. Don't deal with anyone who won't give you his or her name and title, either.
5. Escalate your complaint quickly to higher ups.
6. Speak firmly, with a determined tone in your voice.

7. State that you are unwilling to let the matter be prolonged indefinitely or to repeat your story countless times.
8. Set a reasonable time limit for action — 10 working days is a rule of thumb. If someone appears unable or unwilling to help right away, go above his or her head.
9. Conclude phone calls with a restatement of any agreement that you reach: "So, I can expect delivery by Tuesday?" Or, "I understand that a refund will be mailed to me within a week."
10. Keep clear photocopies or carbons of every letter you send. Successful quality service businesses are very good at "making it right," even by phone. You don't have to fight very hard. Sometimes you will succeed on the phone, but you might also be skillfully put off. (If the person you're speaking with was stricken with a case of total honesty, she or he would say something like: "I don't have time to talk with you now. I have eight other calls waiting.")

So, write a letter.

Send complaint letters directly to decision-makers, primarily to the president of a company. Normally the president will relay your complaint to the person in charge of the department in which the complaint originated.

When an employee receives a letter of complaint that has been forwarded by the president of the company, the message *will* be noticed and *will* be acted upon.

Conclude your letters by requesting a response within a reasonable time, such as two weeks. If you don't hear from anyone by then, send another letter. Ask for details on what's being done about your complaint. Attach a copy of the original letter.

If you don't receive satisfaction to the letter-writing campaign, then set up an appointment to meet with someone, in person.

Whether you have kept paperwork or you must tediously assemble it, send a box full of papers (photocopies only) to your contact, such as a consumer service rep, at the offending company. That person might satisfy your complaint just so he/she can avoid reading your pile of papers!

Or, you might get the same cheery-voiced cooperation *without* sending the papers after you say on the phone: "Why don't I pop up there and show you everything."

When that happens, stop to remind yourself that they could have stonewalled you, flatly refused your request, or shuffled you around until you became discouraged. But, they didn't.

The fact is that *most* companies want you to be satisfied, so sometimes they shortcut what could be a tedious process when they don't have time to deal with a complex complaint. (Who does?) They know that when they give satisfaction to customers the company wins in the long run.

So, give the customer service rep or the department manager a real chance to make things right. We've heard of cases where a customer service rep functioned as a mediator between an angry customer and an employee who quickly regretted his or her actions and apologized.

It's important to begin at lower levels, with the customer service office, for instance, so you can tell higher-ups, with honesty: "I followed procedures."

A reminder: Follow up every meeting (or phone call) with a letter to the person with whom you met or spoke.

If your complaint involves service that disappoints many other people, too, a consumer organization might be eager to help you, and the others. (You *know* that others are frustrated and angry because XYZ Co. is one of the main topics of conversation in your daily lunch group. It ranks right after personal gossip, the weather, and sports.)

A contact with a government consumer protection office, or the Better Business Bureau, can pay off impressively, too. A home improvement contractor who left a pile of insulation pieces, broken studs, smashed sheet rock panels, and nails and screws laying in a home owner's driveway retrieved the junk pile within two hours after a call from a city consumer protection office.

Consumer groups affiliated with city or county government are listed in the phone book among the entries for your city or county offices. To find private consumer groups in your area, see the *Directory of State and Local Consumer Groups* in the library.

For guidance in dealing with the media, see Chapter Sixteen about Action Lines. These TV, radio, and newspaper services accept and investigate complaints from consumers, then report results.

The consumer reporter of a metro TV station obtained refunds for consumers who had been bilked by a basement-waterproofing company. The reporter, acting on tips from consumers, ran stories on the company's practices until the company president was indicted. He was found guilty of consumer fraud and sentenced to prison.

More and more TV stations are setting up these consumer help services, says Silvia Gambardella, consumer specialist at WCCO-TV in Minneapolis. Gambardella does regular on-air reports about consumer complaints and how they were resolved.

CHAPTER 9

EFFECTIVE COMPLAINING: BUSINESS BY BUSINESS

- ❑ Airlines
- ❑ Auto Repair Services
- ❑ Banks
- ❑ Bus Companies
- ❑ Funeral Directors
- ❑ Government
- ❑ Hospitals
- ❑ Lawyers
- ❑ Moving Companies
- ❑ Physicians
- ❑ Railroads
- ❑ Realtors
- ❑ Repair Services
- ❑ Restaurants
- ❑ Retailing
- ❑ Retail Store Delivery
- ❑ Supermarkets
- ❑ Utility Companies

A newspaper carried a columnist's outraged report about the repulsive behavior of the part-owner of a fine new restaurant in a prestigious downtown building.

One of four businessmen arriving for lunch asked to be seated in the back but was told that the space was for guests with reservations.

"But, I have a reservation," the man said.

Mistake. BAD mistake. The retort lit the part-owner's fire.

"If you can't take a joke you can take your (obscenity) out on the street and (obscenity) yourselves."

In a case such as this, the proper reaction probably is to leave. Just leave. That's what the male lunchers did, on their way to another restaurant.

But, for nearly every different rotten-service situation there exists a distinctive reaction that is more effective than other reactions that might occur to you.

AIRLINES

If an airline will not resolve a complaint, write to the Bureau of Consumer Protection, Federal Aviation Administration, Washington, DC 20428. This office will review your complaint to determine if FAA rules have been violated. They'll also tell you what your rights are.

Some disputes must be settled in court, though.

Also send a copy of your complaint, if you wish, to the Aviation Consumer Action Project (ACAP), P.O. Box 19029, Washington, DC 20036, a private consumer organization. It monitors the airline industry. ACAP doesn't resolve individual complaints, but it provides useful information concerning your rights; and the Project supports you in your effort to obtain satisfaction.

To record a complaint with the Department of Transportation, call the Consumer Affairs office at 202-366-2220 or write to Consumer Affairs, Department of Transportation, I-25, Washington, DC 20590. They encourage phone calls, but if you write, include a return address and a daytime telephone number.

AUTOMOBILE REPAIR SERVICES

Pick a mechanic like you pick a surgeon: Get a second opinion. Also, obtain an estimate, even if you must pay for it. Sometimes it's even worth having your car towed out of a shop if you lose confidence in the work being done, instead of paying a $1,000 bill only to have the problem occur again.

Most important of all, says Kenneth Zino, former mechanic who is editor of *Motor* magazine: "Don't be submissive. Be assertive."

"In my experience," says Zino, "women do better than men in dealing with mechanics because they're open. If they don't understand something they ask the mechanic to explain. Men, of course... we know everything about cars. Mechanics tell you it's easier to deceive a man than a woman asking questions."

BANKS

Let's say that you've deposited money in an automatic teller machine on Monday; but when you check on Thursday, the bank knows nothing about it.

You call the bank, give the person you speak with the number on your deposit record, and ask what happened to your money. The employee will tell you that it'll take "10 days," sometimes less, for an investigation. But, you can't wait that long *because you've already written checks* on the amount that you deposited.

So, you call the president's office and explain the problem, even if you can only get the president's secretary. Say that the 10-day policy is unacceptable — that you need your money immediately. She may say: "I'm afraid that's how long it takes. There's a lot of paperwork to go through."

So, *you* say: "Then, please give me the name of an executive who has authority to correct the error and report back to me by tomorrow morning."

You'll most likely get a name.

Now, because dollar signs representing overdraft penalties are swimming around in your head, call the bank executive whose name you were given and tell his or her secretary that you've been referred there by the president's office for fast action on your problem. Explain that you can't be expected to wait for your money when it was the bank, not you, that made an error. Tell the person that if you don't hear back by noon the next day you'll hold the bank liable for all "consequential damages" that you suffer from issuing checks against your "valid deposit." The specter of the bank president hovering over him undoubtedly will move the bank executive you're dealing with to bump your case ahead of other work.

Loss or delay of a deposit is only one of the problems that people have with banks. Long lines is another common banking problem.

If you find yourself waiting endlessly in a long line for one of, let's say, three active tellers when other bank employees are standing around, ask the person behind you to save your place.

Go to the chief teller and ask that another window be opened. If this reasonable request is smilingly ignored, see the manager.

If others in your line look annoyed about spending their lunch hour inching toward their money, you might also want to ask the other waiting customers, in a pleasant but frustrated tone: "Would anyone here help me persuade the manager to open up another teller window?"

Most customers don't like to be the first to complain; but some of them will gladly support *your* effort. The manager who senses an insurrection generally will open one or more teller stations.

For other bank problems, the general rule is to approach bank officers directly.

Officers are insulated from all customers but the largest depositors and borrowers; so, a confrontation with a run-of-the-mill customer is likely to catch the officer's attention and render him or her very cooperative.

BUS COMPANIES

Contact your state's transportation department. Serious complaints that the state transportation department can't or won't handle can be referred to the Interstate Commerce Commission (ICC), Washington, DC 20423, 1-800-424-9312, if the problem involves only interstate service.

FUNERAL DIRECTORS

After you've talked with the owner of the funeral home, contact a local funeral directors' trade association. (Look in the telephone yellow pages under "Associations.") Or, ask any funeral director for the name of the local business association.

The Better Business Bureau can also provide this information.

You might also lodge a complaint with the National Funeral Directors Association of the United States, at 11121 West Oklahoma Avenue, Milwaukee, WI 53227, 414-541-2500.

Or, try the International Order of the Golden Rule, 929 S. 2nd St., Springfield, IL 62704, 217-544-7428, another funeral directors' association.

These groups really do want to police the unprofessional operators in their midst. They might bring down more government scrutiny and regulation upon all of them.

GOVERNMENT

When dealing with government bureaucracy, you always have the advantage of an appointed official who is interested in being reelected. If you get no satisfaction from underlings, a letter to the elected official detailing a legitimate complaint usually will yield instructions to the department you're dealing with to see to it that you receive satisfaction.

Your ultimate weapon, when you've been seriously wronged, is the press. The elected official does not exist who does not fear exposure of his department's callous disregard for the rights of citizens in a Letter to the Editor.

Another effective way to get the attention of the top person in a government agency or department — even when that person is an unelected, hired bureaucrat — is to write a letter in which you tell of your plan to testify before the legislative committee that considers that department's next appropriation request.

This is a practical approach only when the appropriation hearing is near.

To strengthen your threat, include in the letter the actual date and time of the next hearing, if it has been set, or the name, address, and phone number of the agency that will schedule the appropriation hearing.

As far as the bureaucrat knows, you might own your own business or be independently wealthy, so you can afford to take the time needed to testify before a legislative committee.

Even if you are *not* independently wealthy, your outrage might motivate you to *find* time to testify. You may be a salesperson, self-employed, or a worker with access to a day of discretionary time off or a backlog of vacation or sick leave days. Or you may be a homemaker who can juggle your schedule.

Testimony may take no more than an hour if you arrange with a legislative committee or subcommittee chairperson to appear at a specific time.

You might get cold feet, of course; but, meanwhile, the bureaucrat would get cold chills. Next to his own job, the closest thing to a bureaucrat's heart is his department budget.

Be prepared to *carry out the threat* if your letter in which you announce your intention to testify before the appropriations committee goes unanswered and your problem unresolved.

Type out a news release that explains your complaint, alert the press that you will be testifying; and equip the press to report on your testimony by giving them copies of the news release.

Resist the thought that the government department or individual bureaucrat that caused your complaint will retaliate. It is *far* more likely that the person will *not* retaliate. Why? Because your complaint will be a matter of record, making the revenge-minded bureaucrat a logical suspect as the perpetrator of the retaliation.

Generally, the higher you take your complaint in government, the easier it is to fight back successfully.

Elected officials are paying more attention to the people.

If your beef is with the state and underlings are unwilling to take responsibility for your complaint, write to the governor's appointee heading the department. Such people are not career civil servants with the attendant job security. So, they are more likely to be sensitive to constituent complaints.

When you are doing battle with a commission, write to the director and send a copy to all commissioners.

And don't hesitate to write to the governor. In most states the governor's staff will forward your letter to the appropriate department or agency chief. Your complaint letter won't hit the trash can.

But, when you're locked in battle with a front-line government department such as one that handles driver licensing, zoning and planning, public utilities such as streets, curbs, and gutters, or with the dog catcher, *build a file* on the Stubbornly Obstructive Bureaucrat (SOB) — build your case.

You must be able to document your case because some bureaucrats are highly motivated obstructionists, SOBs. Some of them seem to use whatever energy they have to prevent you from getting what you want. Their greatest joy in life seems to derive from the mouthing of the word "No."

Go ahead and feel like a private investigator.

In building your file you'll be given an advantage by those government workers who carelessly convict themselves out of their own mouths. They also lounge about their work places as if they had just dropped in on their way to the country club.

They may be so loose-mouthed and lazy because the Civil Service system makes discharge of a government employee as difficult as bringing a Middle Eastern terrorist to justice.

So, insert in your file names of people you asked for and spoke with. Write down responses such as:

"He's on break now. You can try later."

"He's not back from lunch yet."

"Let me check." Then, five minutes later: "Somebody said he was here, but I can't find him."

"He's gone for the day."

This can go on for weeks...or months.

Incorporate these responses in a letter to the supervisor. Name names. List dates. If you get a response and the response is just another smoke screen, then they've given you more ammunition for a letter to the elected official who is the supervisor's boss.

Covering one specific problem, such a letter might state: "I am sure that you will conclude that I have made every conceivable effort to reach this individual and to resolve my problem with his handling of the important matter that I brought to your department.

"Frankly, I believe that this employee's nonavailability does not meet reasonable standards for public service and does not promote the *efficiency* of your department."

Government, responsible to taxpayers for spending their money wisely, is big on "efficiency."

As a result of your letter, your business probably will be placed in the hands of another employee who certainly will be eager to display greater interest in resolving your original problem.

You are most likely to get the best results at any level of government, however, if you talk to the supervisor privately and explain your problem.

Ask to see the supervisor or agency director. (Remember to jot down the name and employee number of anybody who cold-shoulders you along the way.)

If the people you've been having trouble with try to bar the door to Mr. or Ms. Big, write to Mr. or Ms. Big. Send a copy of your letter to the personnel officers or to the chief administrative officer. Also send a copy to the appointed official who's dependent upon the voters for his or her job.

HOSPITALS

The watchful consumer will keep a Personal Care Log. A log will serve as an effective tool when you demand better service, or if you dispute your bill.

Inconsiderate behavior: We heard of a patient, who happened to be a school superintendent accustomed to giving orders and being obeyed, who was sleeping in his hospital bed at 4 a.m. when a nurse's aide entered his room and...loudly... changed the water in the pitcher beside his bed.

He said nothing. He waited until the nurse's aide left. Then he got up, put his robe and slippers on, shuffled down the hallway to a pay phone, and called the Hospital Administrator at 4:15 a.m.

"I just want to congratulate you on the efficiency of your staff," he told the administrator. The school superintendent's real point was not missed.

Neglect: You ring for a nurse. But, no one comes for 15 minutes. You ring again. And again.

This would be a good entry in your Personal Care Log.

If you're in a double room, enlist the room's other occupant as a witness to poor service you receive. You can serve as witnesses for each other.

LAWYERS

Want to know how to outfox a lawyer? Here are suggested strategies:

1. A lawyer returns your calls days after you phone, or he never calls back. Or, his secretary routinely says that he's in court when you know that some of the time he is not in court. He's just avoiding you.

   A good indication that you're being ignored is when you're not told that the lawyer is out until after you give your name. Ever have that happen?
   It's a breach of professional standards for a secretary to tell you a lawyer's in court when he's sitting at his desk.

From the day of your first consultation or suspected abuse, keep a log of dates and hours that you call your lawyer. Beside the entry, make a notation about the message you conveyed and whether you said the matter was important.

Document your attempts to reach the lawyer in a certified letter to him/her. Be sure to point out that you are aware that he (she) has breached "ethical" standards. Reference to ethics is very motivational for attorneys. They'll often put aside other cases to attend to yours.

An alleged breach of ethical standards is a fine starting point for negotiating new fees.

2. When you call to ask for a document that you were supposed to receive long ago, you're told that it's "in the mail."

   Document the exact time envelopes were postmarked and compare it with the time you called and asked about them. This matching game, brought to your attorney's attention in a brisk letter, will become another damning entry in your log of legal abuses — more fine ammunition for you when fees are discussed.

In general, always complain first to the lawyer, even if you believe that you won't get satisfaction. Doing so *strengthens your case* if you must carry it further.

Only after your lawyer stonewalls you should you pursue a formal grievance against him or her.

Every state has an agency or committee given the power by the state's highest court to handle complaints against attorneys. This agency or committee may be part of the court system or it may be a bar association committee.

The grievance committee may have a booklet or fact sheet that tells you how to complain, so ask.

Grievance committees rarely become involved in fee disputes. If you believe that a lawyer owes you money, sue in small claims court.

MOVING COMPANIES

If you can't thrash out your problem with the crew that moves you, write a detailed, well-reasoned letter to the president of the moving or van line and mail it to company headquarters.

Any reputable company will be fair. But, if you get no response or no satisfaction, call the company's "800" number. Most of them have "800" numbers. For instance:

AERO MAYFLOWER TRANSIT CO., 1-800-428-1200

ALLIED VAN LINES, 1-800-854-3398

NORTH AMERICAN VAN LINES, 1-800-348-2111

UNITED VAN LINES, 1-800-325-3870

Check "Toll Free Directory Assistance" for other moving company "800" numbers. Just dial 1-800-555-1212 on your phone.

Next, contact the watchdogs. If you're moving from city to city within a state, contact the state's Public Utilities Commission (PUC). It probably issued the operating license and has the power to revoke it.

Call the PUC first and follow up with a formal written complaint in which you list your grievances in detail and document them. Also suggest remedies. Pressure from the PUC usually is all it takes to solve a sticky squabble with a moving company.

Once your furnishings and belongings cross the state line, the complaint becomes a federal matter, the jurisdiction of the Interstate Commerce Commission (ICC). The ICC is one of the most responsive and helpful of all federal agencies. It has regional offices in San Francisco, Fort Worth, Chicago, Atlanta, Philadelphia, and Boston. They do handle complaints.

If you wish, write the ICC's Washington headquarters, 12th and Constitution Av. NW, Washington, DC 20243, 1-800-424-9312.

When the ICC calls an interstate mover, the mover jumps. That's because the agency sets interstate moving rates, and it can cancel a mover's operating permit, putting him out of business.

PHYSICIANS

From the time you walk into a doctor's office, he or she has the upper hand. If the waiting room is jammed, you wait. Usually you wait far past your appointment time.

And there's *always* a good explanation. He was called to an emergency at the hospital, perhaps.

But, perhaps he is "overbooking," like airlines do. He schedules more patients than he can handle, just in case some people don't keep their appointments. This way all his time is used — his income maximized.

While you're waiting, the nurse won't even give you a hint of when you'll get in; and she's annoyed that you ask.

Eventually, the nurse ushers you into another room, for *another* wait without even a magazine to read.

The way you are processed by many physicians today is dehumanizing.

A doctor's waiting room is a purgatory where you can waste *hours* to spend *a few minutes* with a doctor who doesn't have time to listen to your report of symptoms.

One of life's greatest satisfactions would surely be to overhear a doctor complaining to an airline ticket agent about being bumped from a flight... because the airline purposely overbooked.

Fight back this way: Ask for appointments early in the morning. If you're the first patient of the day, it's unlikely that you will be kept waiting.

But, the reality is that no matter when you are scheduled to see the doctor, you'll still probably find a waiting room full of people who have been granted appointments at exactly the same time as you!

So, go a step further. When you make your appointment, leave your phone number and ask to be advised of a delay before you leave home. Give the receptionist the time that you will leave.

Unless the doctor is called away on an emergency, the receptionist won't call you. But, you have accomplished one thing, nevertheless: You've begun to establish the basis for the rest of the fight-back plan we'll suggest.

Just before you leave for the doctor's office, phone and confirm the appointment. Then, be prompt...for sure. Don't give the doctor a chance to claim that you didn't show up on time.

Unbeknownst to the doctor, she/he will be playing "beat the clock." Money is being lost every second that ticks by, because for every quarter-hour you wait for him (her) you will deduct from his (her) bill a pro-rated amount equal to *your* hourly pay. You'll almost certainly be kept waiting, despite your planning.

Send your payment with a letter explaining that you were careful to confirm and to be on time and even to request a simple notice of delay; but, still you lost two hours (or whatever the amount of lost time) from your work at an hourly rate of $___. You would like a pro-rated amount, that you specify, deducted from your bill.

This tactic definitely is used by patients. It's not so far-fetched. We've never heard of a case such as this, in which the patient was reasonable, where the doctor refused the requested deduction.

There are other reasons to complain to doctors, as you know. How about the quick going-over that the doctor gives you in his examining room. He's in a hurry, you see.

Don't accept that kind of treatment. Don't let yourself feel that because the doctor is busy you are obliged to tolerate only a quick going-over.

If you are billed the same amount for a fifteen-minute exam as for a three-minute exam, you have something to complain about. You deserve your doctor's *full* attention. Don't settle for anything less.

If you really feel that you didn't get the medical care you paid for, discuss it with your doctor. Again, ask for an adjustment.

Another alternative is to contact your local medical society. Almost all of them have a grievance committee staffed by doctors who want to know about members who are hurting the image of their profession. Some of these committees are kangaroo courts, where the patient has little chance of winning. But, most of them really are fair. Some invite the public to hear grievances and to arbitrate complaints.

RAILROADS

The national network of railroads run by Amtrak has a consumer complaint department for all rail service problems. Contact: Adequacy of Service Bureau, Amtrak, 955 L'Enfant Plaza North, SW, Washington, DC 20024.

REALTORS

If you have a service complaint against a real estate agency or realtor, describe your complaint in a letter to the firm. If the realtor is located in a state different from the state in which the subject transaction took place, send the complaint letter to:

OFFICE OF INTERSTATE LAND SALES REGISTRATION
451 7th Street SW
Washington, DC 20410

Also send the letter to the real estate regulatory agency, if there is one, for the state in which the land is located. These state agencies have various names such as Real Estate Commission, Department of Registration and Education, or Department of State. If you are in doubt as to the right place and the right name, contact the state attorney general's office for the name and address of the proper agency.

REPAIR SERVICES

Dick Youngblood, business columnist for the *Star Tribune* of Minneapolis/St. Paul, thinks that the service economy is a hoax upon the public, as reported earlier. One of the reasons for his belief is that home repair services have not adjusted their service to accommodate the large proportion of homes in which all the occupants are absent during the day. They, too, work only during the day.

If you want your washing machine repaired during the day, you have little recourse other than to stay home and wait for the service company. As a result, you take a loss of pay, in most cases. (You do not wish to risk burglary by leaving your house key under the carpet on the door step.)

But, more home repair services are providing evening and Saturday service, reports MACAP (Major Appliance Consumer Action Panel), an industry-backed organization that mediates service complaints between consumers and major appliance manufacturers.

So, it is less and less necessary to wait at home hoping that the serviceperson will show up when scheduled — or to haul your own washing machine or vacuum cleaner down to the repair shop on your way to work.

Encourage evening and weekend repair service by calling your repair service and suggesting it... *before* you need service.

But, if your problem is a repair service that puts in time, bills you for the time, but doesn't fix the appliance, well, it's time to complain. Start, of course, with the repair service.

If the repair service disagrees with you, approach your local consumer affairs bureau and state attorney general's office.

If the repair shop is a factory-authorized outlet, contact the authorizing manufacturer, too.

If you still can't get results, then go to MACAP. They try to find a mutually satisfactory compromise for consumer complaints. MACAP is located at 20 N. Wacker Dr., Chicago, IL 60606. Phone: 312-236-3165.

Nearly one-third of all households in America experienced at least one *significant* consumer problem during the year before, according to the National Consumer Survey's (NCS) survey sponsored by the U.S. Office of Consumer Affairs. Of households reporting problems, more than 60 percent told of losses averaging $142. Nearly 15 percent of the losses involved lost time from work (waiting for repair people, mainly).

RESTAURANTS

About half the American food dollar is spent in restaurants.

The majority of restaurant owners realize that a sterling reputation takes years to build, but that it can be tarnished in a flash when people start complaining to neighbors, friends, relatives, and co-workers.

So, all you need to do is to threaten to complain...to neighbors, friends, relatives, and co-workers.

But, that strategy doesn't work every time.

In the restaurant business it's practically standard operating procedure (SOP) to maneuver patrons into the bar where they are in a position to buy drinks, thereby adding to the restaurant's revenues for that day.

How often have you heard this: "Wouldn't you like to wait in the bar?"

If you want a drink, fine. But, if you hate being manipulated, take a seat in the lounge but order only a glass of water.

Fifteen minutes past the time of your reservation, tell the maitre d' that you're leaving, tell him why you're leaving... and *go*.

You might end up eating pizza, but at least you'll feel good about yourself for striking a blow for consumer rights. (It won't hurt you to eat pizza once in a while.)

One restaurant reviewer makes an absolutely inspired suggestion for avoiding the bar-herd hassle. Getting a table right away is simple, he says: "Tip the maitre d' when you *arrive*."

Now, why didn't *we* think of that?

Another reviewer (these are very creative people) says that whenever service is slow or sloppy, "I ask the waiter if he's an actor. He's always flattered. Then I say, 'Would you mind acting like a waiter tonight?'" [Nasty, isn't it?]

After you leave a restaurant that's treated you with disrespect, you can always write a clear, unemotional complaint letter to the manager. Sometimes you'll receive a coupon for a free meal.

Go one step farther, if you wish, and send copies of the letter to local restaurant reviewers. Some of them will call the restaurant and maybe even write a story. Most of them will at least file the letter and use it when they receive more complaints about the same restaurant.

Your best revenge, though, is to patronize competitors.

In restaurants, the use of tipping to comment on service is effective. Use tipping both to complain *and* to commend. [TIPS is an acronym for "**T**o **I**nsure **P**rompt **S**ervice.]

If your complaint about poor service isn't satisfied, don't tip. Let the waiter/waitress know why you didn't tip. Look the person in the eye and, without raising your voice, tell him or her that the service was bad and describe exactly what was wrong.

When you tip 15 percent for *bad* service just because the waiter rivets you to the chair with a laser glare, you are endorsing bad service. Tipping when you get bad service is the ultimate cop-out.

If the service was *great*, then tip *more* than 15 percent, if you wish.

RETAILING

Here's a tip on what to do *immediately* when salespeople are argumentative, when they insult your taste, or when they 'serve' you with snail-like deliberation and disinterest.

Don't waste time arguing with a salesclerk. Go to the executive offices and ask to speak to an executive on an "urgent matter." On the way, prepare your case in your mind.

When an executive comes out to meet you, be polite. And be specific. Talk quietly. Convey by word and facial expression that you simply want to obtain the service or merchandise you came in to buy rather than punish the offensive salesperson, even though you wouldn't object if the employee got a dressing down. Say something like:

"I've just spent a good 10 minutes waiting for a salesperson who for all I know is still talking on the phone about her boyfriend, Bobby. I'm not trying to get anyone in trouble, but I *am* trying to buy a sweater and I can't get any help.

"Now, 10 minutes may not seem like a long wait, but it is when you're pressed for time as I am today. I would appreciate it if you would help me get my sweater so I can be on my way."

The executive (let's say the officer is a female) may take you down to the department where you found the sweater that you want to pay for. Her first step will be to find a clerk.

The clerk's colleagues may lie to support the clerk's alibi. But, if you remain calm and avoid name-calling and accusations, the supervisor most likely will believe your account. She realizes that the store actually *does* have an occasional employee who is rude, lazy, and even incompetent.

RETAIL STORE DELIVERY SERVICES

Some businesses assume that once you've waited seven or eight weeks for a delivery, you won't cancel the order and go through the same tiresome experience with another store or manufacturer. So, they become decidedly apathetic.

So, arrange to charge your purchase to your credit account. If you don't have one, open one for this purpose.

When the order signed states delivery will be made in "Four to Six Weeks" and it doesn't arrive on time, some energetic consumers rent the same merchandise such as furniture for use until the purchase arrives. When they receive their statement from the business they bought the merchandise from, they deduct the amount that they paid to rent the furniture. They pay the balance and enclose a note explaining what they've done. They enclose a copy (not the original) of the rental receipt.

The store, of course, will reply in horror, protesting that it's "not our policy" to compensate customers for the inconvenience they cause with their unrealistic delivery dates. They'll say that they can't be held responsible for manufacturer delays.

But, stubbornly refuse to delete compensation for furniture rental from the store's statement. Remind the store's representative that it was the *store* that promised the delivery date, not the manufacturer.

Tell the employee that you'd happily go to court. The fact is that the store really has breached the contract implied in giving a delivery date. A judge probably would find in your favor.

The store representative probably would be smart enough to know that. A judge probably will order the store to allow you to deduct most or all of the disputed amount.

You'll undoubtedly be better off withholding the money and foisting the burden of collection onto the store instead of paying and then suing the store for the amount that you spent renting furniture.

Be sure to send a copy of your letter noting that you've subtracted the cost of rental to the company president. Point out the business's liability and express your willingness to drag the case through the courts, if necessary.

Most presidents decide in favor of closing the books on such matters, if the rental expense isn't overwhelming — larger than the cost of the furniture, for instance.

SUPERMARKETS

Some supermarket managers think they are good businesspeople when they intentionally understaff checkout lines so customers are exposed *longer* to impulse items that line the corridor leading to the checkout counter — items such as Bic lighters, Scotch tape, mini-magazines with horoscope readings, nail clippers, and bubble gum.

But, sometimes supermarkets really are caught short-handed because of illness of checkout personnel. The store has overlooked the need to cross-train other employees so they can fill in at checkout counters.

When lines are long and other checkout registers are going unused, ask a checker to request that another register be opened. If your request falls on deaf ears, summon the manager and ask him or her to have someone open a register.

Usually, that's all it takes. The manager will open a checkout line...and you will be *first* in line.

But, if the manager claims that all the clerks are busy stocking shelves, get assertive: Tell the manager that if he doesn't take care of customers *first*, the clerks won't have to worry about stocking shelves because he'll lose a lot of business once you're through telling your neighborhood how long the lines are in Hinky Dinky Supermarket.

If you're treated *really* inappropriately, and you are *very* angry, threaten to leave your full shopping cart in the checkout aisle and to walk out. The store will need to return your items to the shelves.

Sounds petty, you say? You're right. But, tactics such as this are sometimes justified because they give you, the brow-beaten consumer, much-needed satisfaction and the motivation to continue fighting for service.

These fight-back tactics might lower your blood pressure and save the family dog from assault and battery, too.

When everybody, including the manager, gives you the cold shoulder, there's nothing else you can do but to strike back with a harmless "guerilla tactic." After you leave the supermarket without your groceries, stop off at a convenience store and buy the few items that are absolutely essential. Complete your shopping at a *competitive* supermarket the next day.

UTILITY COMPANIES

If your utility rejects your request for adjustment of an obvious error, contact the local or state Public Service Commission (sometimes called the State Utility Commission).

Send copies of your letters to the company, the utility company's responses, and duplicates of any documentation (bills, meter readings, and so on). This should motivate the commission to investigate.

If the State Utility/Public Service Commission doesn't get very far, you can ask the Commission to mediate your case.

The first step usually is an *informal* mediation hearing. If that doesn't resolve the matter, you may receive a *formal* hearing with a referee assigned by the Commission. Most complaints are settled before they reach this point, however.

Your state might also have a Consumer Advocacy Office for utility complaints.

If you strike out with the Utility/Public Service Commission, contact the National Association of State Utility Consumer Advocates (NASUCA) to find out if your state has such a "utility consumer advocate." Reach NASUCA at: Florida Public Council, 202 Blount St., Rm. 624, Crown Bldg., Tallahassee, FL 32301. Phone: 904-488-9330.

CHAPTER 10

LIGHTS, ACTION... COMPLAIN!

"The First Rule: Personalize"

When a service employee is rude or incompetent, tell him or her about it. But, don't hold your breath while you wait for an apology and satisfaction. After all, you're confronting the person who has caused your problem. This person is likely to become defensive.

The logical first step is to see the manager of the perpetrator of the service problem, at once. If you strike out with the manager, immediately obtain an appointment with the manager's boss.

A personal meeting is an effective ploy. You'll be talking privately, face-to-face. It's difficult for anyone to say "No" when you are bearing down with close eye contact.

Look the person in the eye, explain the problem, and ask: "Can you help me?"

Remember that your attitude and personal demeanor are important in a personal meeting. Act confident of your facts and figures and of the position you've taken.

And don't approach the person you're meeting with hat in hand and eyes downcast.

You are demanding a right. Your complaint is legitimate.

So, act as if you fully expect satisfaction.

The customer is boss.

Chapter 11

LIGHTS, ACTION... COMPLAIN!

"The Second Rule: Be Persistent"

Businesspeople find it difficult to rebuff a persistent customer. They're inhibited by a soft voice that says: "It's bad business to say 'No' to a customer."

So, persistence is the ace up your sleeve.

Here are examples of persistence.

CASE: A Chatsworth, California, auto repair shop failed to lubricate the wheel bearings during brake servicing on George Anderson's van. It was an oversight that a certain screeching noise made quite evident. As he drove the van back to the shop, the rear axle twisted off.

The repair shop refused to repair the axle at no cost; so he was forced to tow the van to another garage where he paid $2,000 to have the work done.

That made him mad. So, for eight months he parked his motor home on the street in front of the repair shop. He decorated it with gaudy signs that accused the repair shop of shoddy workmanship.

Anderson had the same sharply worded messages printed on T-shirts and buttons that he wore constantly. And he painted the messages on protest signs that his friends carried outside the shop.

He hired a lawyer to help him pursue a claim against the auto repair shop. But he fired the attorney when he told Anderson to take his "libelous" signs off the side of the van.

Eventually he won what he sought: The national franchisor of the Chatsworth shop agreed to pay Anderson $5,200 to reimburse him for the cost of axle repairs to his van, for a new paint job, and for damage from a break-in to the vehicle when it was parked outside the Chatsworth shop while mechanics debated who was at fault for the axle damage.

What's more, the company promised to handle complaints from 30 strangers who had stopped and told Anderson stories of their own bad repair experiences with the shop.

CASE: Robert Imboden of El Toro, California, is typical of nearly 100 consumers who complained to the Orange County district attorney about Arthur M. Shubin, owner of Sante Fe Springs Carpet & Upholstery Steam Cleaning.

For $6.50, his ads read, he would steam-clean the carpeting in one room — $31.95 for five rooms. The ads were thick with appealing offers: "No hidden charges" and "Free spot removing and pre-manual scrubbing."

Two Shubin employees named Pat and Jose came to Imboden's home to clean the carpet, Imboden said in a court declaration. But Pat told Imboden and his wife that the carpet was much too dirty to be cleaned for the advertised price. It must be "preconditioned," they said — for $99.50.

All of the other complainants said they were told the same thing — that their carpets were too dirty for the low price and that they had to be "preconditioned."

But, Imboden insisted that he wanted the $6.50-per-room price.

"Fine," said Pat. "It'll take us less than 10 minutes to do all five rooms."

"It did not seem possible that they could spot-clean, manually pre-scrub and steam-clean 900 square feet of carpet in that time," Imboden said later.

So, he ordered them to leave. When they insisted on a $10 service fee, he called police.

One woman told the court that after the $6.50 quickie, she complained to Shubin about the poor quality of the work.

"You get what you pay for, lady," she was told.

Wendy Brough, Orange County deputy district attorney, took Shubin to court and put him out of business.

"Shubin's was a classic bait and switch," Brough said. "You advertise one price, then use high-pressure tactics to try to force the consumer into something more expensive."

Persistence pays. If these consumers had limited expression of their indignation to yelling at employees, they'd still be yammering to friends about their bad experiences.

Whatever you do, don't give up too soon.

Chapter 12

How to Write "The Letter"

"There's a fly in my McNuggets."

In large companies, where employees commonly pore over customer letters that are written in anger and letters that are boring, vague, abusive, handwritten on grocery bags, and longer than the Holy Bible, you have to make your letter *stand out.*

Be creative.

A Pennsylvania housewife sent Ford Motor Co. Customer Relations department a 12-page comic book... original, done by her own hand. It illustrated the saga of repair problems with her Ford Pinto and how it had strained her marriage. The Customer Relations department returned its own hand-drawn comic book called "Captain Pinto to the Rescue."

Ford fixed the car, for nothing.

Another consumer typed his complaint on toilet tissue and sent the roll to the customer service department. Since he maintained his sense of humor and avoided anger and insult in the letter, the company's servicepeople responded with a humorous letter in which they promised to satisfy his complaint.

A woman wrote to General Electric Company repeatedly to tell the company that her new iron didn't work. All she got in return was form letter after form letter.

Disgusted, she eventually put the iron in a paper bag, scrawled on it "IRON NO GET HOT" and mailed it to G.E. She got a new iron for her creative communication.

FOLLOW UP MEETINGS WITH LETTERS

If a letter that you write earns you a meeting, write another letter, right after the meeting, in which you review all the promises and statements made during the meeting. Send it to your primary contact. This letter becomes a record of the meeting.

Include the first and last names of every person in addition to the addressee that you have dealt with at the company, including those you saw during your personal visit.

Name anyone who promised to get back to you and specify the deadline date that was given for response.

A follow-up letter should include:

- ❑ Your name
- ❑ Your address
- ❑ Your home and work phone numbers
- ❑ Date and place of purchase
- ❑ Specific statement of your complaint
- ❑ Brief history of the problem
- ❑ Copies of all pertinent documents. (Do not send originals.)

If you want repair service, include name and model and serial number of the product to be repaired.

Be sure to avoid angry statements. Anger is counterproductive: It *lowers* your chances for satisfaction, instead of increasing your chances.

TYPE THE LETTER (IF POSSIBLE)

Most businesses, eager to hear from their customers, are unconcerned about whether a letter is typed or not. And they won't give you a poor grade because of spelling errors. Of course, companies consist of human beings who find it easier to read typed letters, so they *prefer* them. Most progressive companies will not neglect a letter just because it is handwritten, though.

Make two copies of your letter, whether you type it or not. If you don't have a typewriter, perhaps your local library has coin-operated typewriters and you can use one of them.

It's important that you keep copies of every letter or handwritten note so you can either duplicate them or use them as guidance for future letters: You never know how many letters you'll be sending.

AN EFFECTIVE LETTER

You are most likely to be satisfied with your letter's results when you:

1. Begin with a compliment. Emphasize your satisfaction with the business...until now.

2. Identify the service you're complaining about. If the bad service includes a purchase, identify the product with serial, model or service numbers. State where the transaction took place and include a copy of the receipt.

3. Describe precisely why you are dissatisfied.
4. Explain what you'd like the company to do.
5. Close with a pleasant request for assistance.

Near the beginning of a letter, after the complimentary comment, include specifics such as: "This letter is a request for credit of $250 on my account (Account No. 000-00-0000) as a result of non-delivery of a woman's coat purchased Dec. 4, 1992, at your Peoria branch."

Don't get sidetracked into long explanations about how the problem came about. You'll just confuse the service rep. Simply describe the problem. There's no need to report that the store nearly ruined your sister's wedding because the bridesmaids' shoes were dyed mauve instead of peach.

Be sure to specify what you *want.*

- ❑ "I want the cost of the coat plus tax credited to my account."
- ❑ "I want the finance charges of $13 removed from my bill."
- ❑ "I want to cancel the order."

On every piece of correspondence, include name, address, day-time phone number, and your account number in the upper right corner so that you and your problem can be quickly identified.

A letter should include everything that a business needs to act immediately. If they have to search for this information in their records, or call you for more information, the response you desire will be delayed.

Include a clear copy of receipts for any service or merchandise.

WHAT THE TEACHER SAYS ABOUT LETTER-WRITING

Gayle Knutson teaches a class on writing effective consumer letters. It's entitled "There's a Fly In My McNuggets and Other Consumer Letters." These are some of her points:

- ❑ Make the complaint letter short and to the point. Explain the problem, when you noticed it, what you did to correct it, and what you want the merchant or manufacturer to do. Be confident, not emotional or hostile.
- ❑ Specify all important facts such as date and place you made the purchase and any information that identifies the product, such as the serial or model number. If you are writing to complain about a service, describe the service and who performed it.
- ❑ Type your letter. If you write it, be sure that it is neat and easy to read.
- ❑ Send copies of receipts, not originals. (We've made this point earlier.) Gather evidence in a file folder — sales receipt, warranty, repair or service orders, canceled checks, contracts, and correspondence. If the complaint involves shoddy workmanship, take photographs that display the workmanship.
- ❑ Begin at the origin of your complaint and move upward from there toward the top executive. If your problem is with a service provided by a professional (doctor, lawyer, funeral director, accountant), your best bet may be to complain to the state board that licenses the person if the individual doesn't solve the problem.

ADVICE FROM ON HIGH

Here are letter-writing tips from Richard Viguerie. You may recognize his name. He's the magician who raised millions of dollars for conservative political causes and campaigns, largely with powerfully persuasive letters.

A lead paragraph, says Viguerie, should be brief — no more than two sentences of 10 to 12 words each.

Begin with an opening statement such as: "I have a problem and I need your help." Then, summarize the problem in a dramatic way, also in the first paragraph. For example: "I am very distressed by a billing error that your company refuses to correct."

In the second paragraph, spring a surprise. *Compliment* the company! (Earlier we suggested a compliment in the *first* paragraph. Take your choice.)

Mix the sweet with the sour, says Viguerie. You might try: "Over the years I've been very happy with your service. Every time I entered your store a salesperson would ask within a minute or two if they could help me."

In the next paragraph, go for the kill: "So, you can imagine my dismay when I went searching for a salesperson after waiting 10 minutes and found three of them in an intimate conversational huddle, totally unresponsive to customers."

Move on to detail. Omit *unnecessary* details.

Here's a letter that contains the required detail: "On August 12 an employee, John Smith, in your Cornucopia store spent approximately 10 minutes with another employee discussing a party the previous night while I waited to ask where I could find an electric meat knife. I interrupted once and was told to 'Wait a minute.'

"This is the third time in a month that I've found it very difficult to get service in your store. It's not necessary for me to put up with rude and indifferent service when I can easily switch my business to Smilin' Jack's Emporium — which is exactly what I am considering."

Since most people only scan a letter, present your request twice so they are less likely to miss it. The second sentence of the first paragraph and again at the end would do nicely.

Keep your letter short. If you can't keep it to one page, number important points so the letter is easy to follow.

Don't produce an angry three-page, single-space letter. Customer service representatives find long letters to be intimidating and time-consuming. As a result, too often they put aside a legitimate complaint for attention "next Monday."

It's a good idea to let someone else read the letter before you mail it. If that person thinks the message is clear, then the person who receives it probably will comprehend it, also.

FIVE ELEMENTS

A good letter consists of five simple elements, whether you are just "calling your attention to"" or saying "I think somebody ought to be aware of..." They are:

1. Clear statement of problem. "You mistakenly debited my account $1,200."

2. Facts that back up the story.

3. Request for redress: Correction of a bill. Refund. Repairs. Or, if you're merely ticked off about bad service, request an apology.

4. Deadline for resolution of your problem.

5. A warning of further action that will be taken if things don't go your way.

This "warning of further action" is effective. Here are suggested actions to use:

- ❑ "I'm going to stop payment." If you carry out this threat the company either will negotiate or sue. By law *it cannot blacken your credit record* or sic collection agencies on you until you admit that you owe money to the firm or until a judge or jury decides that you owe money.
- ❑ "I'm going to spend my money elsewhere." Confirming the effectiveness of this warning, the head of the customer relations department for Bloomingdale's department store in York said: "If a customer spends a lot of money in the store, I'll try to settle a complaint right away."
- ❑ "I'll tell everybody who'll listen about your bad service." Dissatisfaction with a merchant or manufacturer spread by word of mouth kills sales.

Recently, a Boy Scout leader called a Safeway supermarket to protest video games that he viewed as a corrupting influence. His threat (which was spoken, but could have been part of a letter) was: "To mobilize my Troop to picket the store."

The vision of a troop of Boy Scouts marching in front of a Safeway persuaded company executives to remove the machines.

When dealing with utilities, your best threat is to say that you'll take your complaint to a higher authority — to an industry association, to the Better Business Bureau, or to state public service commission, the government regulatory body that approves rate increases.

Don't threaten a utility company with the public service commission until you've written the company president. All you need to do to get his/her name, in most cases, is to call the company and ask for it.

Don't send copies of a letter to anyone other than the contact at the company you're complaining to. Most of the time you will get satisfaction. On the few occasions when you are stonewalled, then you should send your letter to state and local consumer protection agencies and others.

FOLLOW-UP LETTER

Follow up an initial letter with a second letter when a company ignores you or refuses your request. This time, threaten action such as sending copies of the letter to 50 of your friends and relatives.

If you feel guilty for making threats, remind yourself that you are helping other consumers who are too timid to complain, and you are helping companies that need *satisfied* consumers to stay in business.

You may feel better if you just *imply* a threat, as consultant John McMullen. He worked for a subsidiary of what was formerly Control Data Corporation (CDC).

McMullen found that his bags hadn't arrived at the airport when he did. In one of the missing bags was his business suit. He needed it for an important meeting in an hour. He had to rush over to a nearby men's store and buy a suit and accessories.

After his meeting, he went to see the airline's manager at the airport. With a condescending air the manager ordered a check for $25.

When McMullen reached home, he sent a letter to the airline noting that he'd sent a copy to Frank Borman, then president of the airline, and to the "CDC Travel Service."

The person who read the letter may have assumed that the travel service, which was *fictitious*, schedules hundreds of flights each year for CDC executives: A check for the full amount of McMullen's purchases arrived within days.

LETTER TO THE PRESIDENT

It's true that it is effective to write letters to the president or to the chairman of a company.

Letters to presidents are effective because they pass the letters on to the consumer affairs/customer service departments — and the people in those departments give royal treatment to letters sent down by the president.

Another good reason to write the company president is that a complaint letter probably will startle him or her. Subordinates, you see, send the president a lot of good news. But, bad news often is pigeonholed. The president might be alarmed to learn that some customers are not overcome with gratitude for the consistently stellar service they receive. He might even pen an order note on your letter as he forwards it to the customer service manager.

The president, after all, has a greater stake in the success of the business than anyone.

Don't be stymied if you don't know the president's name and address. Call the company and ask for it. Consult *Standard & Poor's Register of Corporations, Directors and Executives* or *Thomas' Register of American Manufacturers*, mentioned earlier. They are available in most libraries.

If the corporation that runs the business isn't listed in either directory, then it's an obscure company or very new. Tell your friendly reference librarian what you want and she most likely will find the information somewhere else.

When the parent corporation's name differs from the name of the company you deal with, and when its name or address are not displayed on signs, letterheads, and receipts... then ask the store manager's office for the parent corporation's name so you can look up address and president's name. (Try asking for his name and address, to avoid the need to look it up.)

If you know that the parent corporation is in your town, look for it in the phone book. Call and ask the name of the president.

Say to the operator, in a pleasant voice: "I need to write a letter to the president. Will you give me the name and address, please?"

In most cases she'll give you the president's name. If she doesn't, then alternate measures are called for. A few hours later, after the operator most likely has forgotten your first call, try again with a little different approach. "I am writing a letter to the president and I want to be sure to spell the name correctly. Will you give me the correct spelling of the president's name, please?"

You are implying that you already know his name and that you are just checking for the correct spelling. But, when the operator spells the name, that's when you will be learning it.

All businesses committed to quality service want to know about service problems. They realize that they can't correct a problem unless they know that it exists.

Consumers ought to avoid the automatic belief that all bad service is intentional and that it is caused by a malicious attitude toward customers. A business would be crazy to consistently court customer *dis*satisfaction.

Consider the likelihood that a business doesn't know when it has problems, that front-line employees frequently (conveniently) "forget" to report complaints to supervisors, and that supervisors rarely report complaints to management. This is exactly what happens unless a company happens to have a well-established customer service program that motivates front-line employees to practice good service.

A complaint to a customer service department, to supervisors, or to the president is a service by *you* that the vast majority of companies appreciate. Don't hesitate to complain because you think that you might make somebody "mad."

Stay calm, present the facts, ask for satisfaction, and you'll get it, most of the time.

The customer *is* the boss.

CHAPTER 13

LETTER SAMPLES

How to create a quality letter.

Positive Statement
Problem
Supporting Facts
Action Requested

Here are samples of letters that employ the principles discussed in Chapter Twelve. You may be able to use the letters just as they are, after inserting facts related to *your* case, such as your name and address. Locate points at which words and phrases should be replaced with information specific to your case.

AIRLINE: DELAYED LUGGAGE; POOR SERVICE

July 19, 19__

Mr. Smiley Seducia
Director of Customer Service
Albatross Airlines
120 Decibels Dr.
Wheaton, NI 00004

Dear Mr. Seducia:

POSITIVE STATEMENT

I've flown your airline three times a month for the past nine years and I have always been satisfied. But now I have a problem. I hope you can help.

DATE/PLACE

My luggage was lost on my past two flights, Flight 5227 from Chicago to New York, March 10, and Flight 624 from Chicago to Miami, March 21.

PROBLEM

The luggage did not arrive at my hotel until several hours after I arrived. I had to buy a swim suit to replace the one in the luggage. A receipt for $15.90 is enclosed. I expect payment.

The prospect of having only the clothes on my back during two days of business meetings in New York was a great inconvenience.

The luggage didn't arrive until I'd already bought a clean shirt, socks, and underwear for the second day. There was no way that I was going to send my only clothes to the hotel's laundry and risk not getting them back in time to wear them my second day in New York. The bill, this time, was $47.93, enclosed. Please send reimbursement.

SUPPORTING FACT

Another manifestation of bad service is that in neither New York nor Miami did your airline deliver my luggage. In both cases my hotel picked up the luggage. These incidents indicate to me that your standard of service has slipped.

CONSTRUCTIVE CRITICISM

I suggest that you look into this matter before you alienate a large proportion of your customers.

I hope that these incidents of lost luggage and lack of interest in rectifying the problems you cause are temporary departures from your usual good service.

PLEASANT REQUEST FOR RESPONSE

Please, however, send reimbursement for my expenses.

Sincerely,

ATTORNEY GRIEVANCE

Sample Letter to Bar Association Grievance Committee

July 13, 19__

Mr. Albert Plummet, Esq.
Slip, Fall and Lacerate, Ltd.
Ambulance, MU 00007

Dear Sirs:

HISTORY On January 24, 19 __, I retained the firm of Larson and Mason, Esq., to draft a pre-nuptial agreement. As you can see from the retainer agreement, attached, the fee was to be $500. The amount was paid on the date that the firm was retained.

PROBLEM Once the firm obtained the fee it seems that they lost interest in performing the work. The telephone record and record of letters mailed to Larson and Mason, enclosed, show that I contacted them an average of once a week, beginning in March, asking for the agreement.

PROBLEM The pre-nuptial agreement arrived at my home yesterday, but since I was married in June, the pre-nuptial agreement now is post-nuptial. What's more, now that we are married my wife refuses to sign an agreement — pre or post.

ACTION REQUESTED I wish to submit this case to your panel for fee arbitration. (Frankly, I feel that I owe nothing because I did not receive a pre-nuptial agreement post haste.) Please forward to me any forms that you need to process this case.

PLEASANT CONCLUSION Thank you for your help.

Yours truly,

AUTOMOBILE SERVICE

Letter to Automotive Dealer

April 10, 19__

Mr. Big Squeeze, President
Lemon Motor Car Co.
Wassahatchie, KT 99008

Dear Mr. Squeeze:

POSITIVE STATEMENT

I've been a customer of your service department for about 15 years, as you may know. Usually I've been satisfied with your work. This letter expresses my first complaint.

SUPPORTING FACTS

Six weeks ago today you finished repairs to the left front fender of my car. However, you did not replace the grill because, you said, you could not obtain the part for another two weeks. I needed the car, so I took it without the grill. Another six weeks to the day after you finished repairing the fender you still have not replaced the grill.

I could be wrong, but grills for late model cars can't be that difficult to find. If you had not begun this repair job and left it unfinished, I might be inclined to locate a grill myself. I'm sure that I could find one at a used auto parts yard. As you know, body parts from auto parts yards usually are in good condition.

ACTION REQUESTED

I'm asking you to get more serious, to exert more honest effort to find a grill, and to install it in my car. If you don't, you will, Mr. Squeeze, lose a long-time customer. And that is not the kind of thing that should reassure you about the long-term future of your firm.

PLEASANT REQUEST FOR RESPONSE

Thank you for your cooperation. I expect to hear from you within a week that you want my car in your service department so you can replace the grill.

Very truly yours,

BANK ERROR

November 31, 19_

Mr. Phillippe Conceete
Manager
Bank of Philanthropy
2222 Forked Tongue St.
Generosity, GT 80809

Dear Mr. Conceete:

POSITIVE OPENING

I have been a customer of your bank for five years, and I have always been treated well.

SUPPORTING FACTS/ BACKGROUND INFROMATION

But, now I must complain about your failure to credit a $376.97 deposit that I made October 13. I have lost the receipt for that deposit, however.

Perhaps years of experience with deposits being faithfully credited made me careless. But, non-existence of a deposit slip has no bearing upon your ability to locate an excess in your balance for October 13.

COMPLAINT SPECIFICS

I can no longer accept your claim that the excess does not show up in your records. Authorities that I have consulted tell me that the most likely reason that you haven't found the excess is that you haven't looked for it. Apparently you feel that customer satisfaction is not important.

It's not surprising that you are very efficient at billing me for payments on loans. It is surprising, though, that you can't seem to correct an error when you owe money to me.

REQUEST FOR ACTION

If you can't find my $376.97 I will close my account.

Sincerely,

BANK: POOR SERVICE

October 17, 19__

Mr. Robert George, President
Third Bank of West River
Gasbaggio, PM 00001

Re. Acct. No. 1A2S3D4F

Dear Mr. George:

POSITIVE STATEMENT

I have a problem and I need your help.

Your service has been helpful for the seven years that I've been a customer. But that's changed.

DATE/PLACE OF SERVICE

On October 10, my brother was hit by a motorcycle as he was riding his unicycle. He was rushed to the Emergency Ward of Wellness General Hospital, but the hospital wouldn't admit him unless he deposited $2,000, since he had no insurance.

SUPPORTING FACTS

My brother called and asked if he could borrow the money from me. I rushed to the nearest branch, Dogpatch Branch, though I bank at the main bank, only to discover when I arrived that I'd forgotten my checkbook. I intended to write out a check to obtain cash from my checking account.

COMPLAINT HISTORY

Your cashier, Sally Insipid, ID No. 777, insisted that she could not give me a counter check to use, though I had plenty of valid identification. She said that your computer was not working and that she was too busy to make a phone call to the main bank.

Repeated appeals, citing my brother's need, failed to budge good Ms. Insipid.

BUSINESS BENEFIT

I have not bounced a single check in seven years, and I have repaid each of two loans on time. You have had nearly $100,000 of mine to invest for your benefit. I feel that I deserved better treatment.

PLEASANT CONCLUSION

I hope that you see that it is in your interests to correct a clear and significant customer relations problem that exists in the attitude of Ms. Insipid, and probably in attitudes of other cashiers, assuming that they share the same principles.

Sincerely,

APPLIANCE REPAIR SERVICE: NON-PERFORMANCE

June 30, 19__

Mr. Oscar Boxer
AAAA Appliance Repair Service
447 Someday Av.
Jeopardy, IM 00009

Dear Mr. Boxer:

COMPLAINT I waited all morning on Tuesday, June 28, for your service person to show up to repair my washing machine. He didn't come and he didn't call to say that he wouldn't be coming.

COMPLAINT HISTORY This is the second day that this has happened. The first day, one week ago, I was able to take paid time off from work. This time I was not paid; so I lost income.

EXPANSION OF COMPLAINT I live in your service area and I still want to do business with you. The question is, do you want to do business with me? If you do, what action by you do you propose as compensation for the needless loss of pay that you have caused me?

ACTION REQUESTED Please give me your response. My phone number at work is 909-0909. My home phone number is 808-0808.

Very truly yours,

REQUEST FOR INTERVENTION

A letter to a business association when a contractor fails to live up to terms of a contract.

July 5, 19__

National Home Improvement Council (NHIC)
11 East 44th St.
New York, NY 10017

RE: Stringer Construction, Inc.
447 Surly Av.
Crooked, IM 00009

Gentlemen:

PROBLEM Stringer Construction, Inc. and I have an ongoing dispute over the company's compliance with the enclosed contract between us.

COMPLAINT HISTORY I have also enclosed a day-to-day log that contains digests of my conversations with Stringer's representative and actions I've taken to induce the company to do the work it promised.

ACTION REQUESTED Stringer is a member of NHIC, thereby subscribing to your Code of Ethics. I would appreciate it if you would prevail upon the company to live up to its agreement.

REQUEST FOR RESPONSE Please let me know the result of your discussion of this problem with Stringer.

Very truly yours,

cc: Stringer Construction, Inc.

COMPLAINT TO A BONDING COMPANY

July 5, 19__

Mr. Roger Gotrocks
Easymoney Bonding Company
Miami Beach, FL 00008

RE: Poor Richard's Construction, Inc.

Dear Mr. Gotrocks:

BACKGROUND

You are the surety for Poor Richard's Construction, Inc., according to my state Home Improvement Commission. As part of your surety bond you have agreed to cover losses caused by defective work of Poor Richard's, according to the Commission.

COMPLAINT HISTORY

I may be forced to bring suit against Poor Richard's for non-performance of a contract between us. The company has refused to do work that they were contracted to do.

ACTION REQUESTED

If you wish to avoid a claim by Poor Richard's on their surety bond with you, I suggest that you use your influence to persuade the company to comply with the terms of our contract.

Very truly yours,

cc: Poor Richard's Construction, Inc.

EMPLOYEE MISCONDUCT

December 11, 19__

Mr. Peter Randolph, President
Bottomline Department Store
Dogpatch, RC 00005

Dear Mr. Randolph:

POSITIVE OPENING For many years I have been sufficiently satisfied with your service to continue spending several thousand dollars each year at your store. But, now I am afraid that I must express dissatisfaction with Bottomline Department Store.

PROBLEM I wish to report a serious case of customer abuse by employees in the Ready-to-Wear Dresses department.

SUPPORTING FACTS I stood in the department for a full 15 minutes yesterday before an employee offered to assist me. During that time several employees walked by me, without speaking. Off to one side two young female employees were stocking shelves and carrying on a laugh-and-giggle personal conversation.

The salesperson who eventually approached was very patronizing and condescending. Her name was Ms. Porous. Because I didn't know exactly the style and color I wanted, Ms. Porous treated me with great impatience.

When I asked questions she tossed off incomplete answers in a rude tone. I got the impression she was just trying to get rid of me.

CONSTRUCTIVE CRITICISM Mr. Randolph, I'm sure that you realize that customers are the only reason that you have a store, and a bank account.

ACTION REQUESTED I still feel decidedly insulted by the treatment I received from Ms. Porous. Can you assure me that steps will be taken to prevent rude and unhelpful behavior by your employees in the future?

May I hear from you by January 3?

Very truly yours,

HOTEL SERVICE

January 29, 19__

Mr. Samuel Suave
General Manager
Midtown Hotel
2020 Boondoggle Blvd.
Old York, OY 10017

Dear Mr. Suave:

POSITIVE OPENING

I'm sure that you receive many compliments on the beauty of your hotel and the fancy uniforms that your employees wear. But, has anybody done you the favor of suggesting improvements?

COMPLAINT BACKGROUND

I will. I have two complaints.

First, one hour elapsed between the time I phoned in my room service order on January 23 at 6:20 p.m. and the time that I received it at 7:20 p.m.

Second, that same day, when I returned to my room after an absence of four hours, I found that the bed had not been made or the room cleaned, and there were cigarette butts in the ash tray. That's a significant point, since I don't smoke.

ACTION REQUESTED

I will give you one more chance, Mr. Suave. I hope that you will be able to "light a fire" under your kitchen and housekeeping staffs and that you will teach housekeeping employees not to smoke in the rooms. The rooms might be occupied by non-smokers. I am a non-smoker.

ACTION INTENDED

If I experience more bad service on my next trip, I will take my business across the street on my frequent visits to your city. And I will advise the travel director for my company to avoid this hotel when scheduling trips for our executives.

Sincerely,

INSURANCE BROKER: CLAIM SETTLEMENT

March 3, 19__

Mr. Will Wrong
99 Poor House Lane
Overinsured, AT 00005

Dear Mr. Wrong:

POSITIVE STATEMENT

You have been my insurance agent for nine years, Mr. Wrong. I have a problem that I hope you can help me with.

COMPLAINT

As you know, I bought homeowners insurance from Able Insurance Co. upon your recommendation. I relied on your professional judgment, alone, in deciding to buy the policy from Able.

COMPLAINT HISTORY/ PROBLEM

You told me that this company has a reputation for timely claim settlements. But, I've learned from the (name of your state) Insurance Department that Able has the worst record of any company in terms of complaints per premium dollars collected.

This is relevant because I've been trying to collect on a claim for six months without success. A 50-foot oak tree fell on my garden shed during the 19__ Labor Day hurricane *while I was inside of it.* Half the building was demolished — the half that I was *not* in.

SUPPORTING FACTS

But Able claims that the damage to my house was due to my negligence in building the garden house where the tree fell. Can you believe it? Documents that support my assertion that the company refused to pay my claim are enclosed.

PROBLEM

I feel that I have been damaged by relying upon your advice, since Abel refused to pay what I consider to be a reasonable claim.

ACTION REQUESTED

I urge you to use your influence with this company to persuade the firm to honor my claim. Can you resolve this matter within 10 days?

Very truly yours,

LATE DELIVERY

March 27, __

Mr. Otto Orsini, President
Fatwood Furniture Co.
3636 Ottomon Av.
Etagere, MP 00002

RE: Contested Charge
Breach of Contract
Charge Account No. 222-33-99

Dear Mr. Orsini:

DATE/PLACE OF SERVICE

On February 13, 19__, I bought a bedroom set from you, charging the $962 cost to my account.

COMPLAINT HISTORY

On the sales slip your salesperson wrote: "Delivery week of March 7 to 13." That delivery date was acceptable because the apartment I was furnishing was to be occupied on March 15.

The furniture did not arrive when promised, however. So it was necessary for me to rent a bedroom set for my tenant. The bedroom set arrived yesterday, 14 days later than promised.

PROBLEM

It is basic in the law that a contract is formed when an offer is accepted. You made an offer to deliver the furniture and I accepted the offer by signing my credit card slip.

Then you breached an existing contract by failing to deliver the furniture when promised. Your breach of the contract was the proximate and foreseeable cause of my rental expenses of $58.

Your billing department says that Fatwood Furniture is not responsible for my rental costs because your manufacturer did not deliver the furniture to you in time for you to deliver it to me at the appointed time.

Please understand that the contract was between you and me. The manufacturer was not mentioned in our contract. Legally, the contract was with *you*, and *you* breached it.

ACTION REQUESTED

I expect you to correct my billing and credit me for the $58 rental fee.

Yours truly,

MOVING COMPANY: LATE ARRIVAL AND DAMAGE

June 27, 19__

Mr. Stanley Strangelove
Executive Customer Service Representative
Bump-and-Grind Moving Co.
Slow Motion, IE 00004

Dear Mr. Strangelove:

POSITIVE STATEMENT Your employees all were very cordial during our recent move. That's why I am sorry to enter a claim against Bump-and-Grind.

COMPLAINT The claim is for inconvenience and damages caused by your overdue delivery of my home furnishings and damage to furniture.

DATE/PLACE On June 3, your company's van left our Okefenokee, MU, home on its way to Wasahatchie, TP. It did not arrive until June 8, though you had scheduled it to arrive on June 5.

That left my wife, my two children, and myself with no place to stay except a motel for three nights more than we expected.

SUPPORTING FACTS I'm sure that you know that the law requires you to cover an inconvenience claim for food and lodging. Such a claim, with receipts as documentation, is attached.

Enclosed also is an appraisal by Sterling & Tiffany, Inc., of the gouges made by a sharp instrument in my antique roll-top desk.

ACTION REQUESTED I expect your check for $2,222.22 in settlement of both claims within 30 days.

Sincerely,

PHYSICIAN OVERCHARGE

December 23, 19__

Dr. Francois Flawless
3 Malpractice Sq.
Mercedes Benz, Fl 11990

Dear Dr. Flawless:

BACKGROUND I've been a patient of yours for almost three years.

POSITIVE STATEMENT During that time I've had many an occasion to mention your friendly, competent manner to my acquaintances. I have never been dissatisfied with you before.

PROBLEM However, I must complain about an obvious overcharge.

COMPLAINT HISTORY Did you really intend to charge me $60 for a three minute office visit? Absolutely *all* that you did was to ask me how I felt and then write out a prescription for what turned out to be a case of the flu.

ACTION REQUESTED I feel fine, now. But I will surely have a relapse — an emotional relapse — unless you reduce this bill by half, or more. Thank you.

Sincerely,

RENTAL CAR

June 17, 19__

Mr. Roger Goforit
Timely Car Rental, Inc.
2222 Languid Dr.
Thermopolis, GR 29299

Dear Mr. Goforit:

POSITIVE STATEMENT

Your automobiles are clean and your service is timely...most of the time.

COMPLAINT BACKGROUND

But slow service cost me dearly last week. Because it took your employees at Dogpatch International Airport *20 minutes* to process me when I returned a car and another 20 minutes to get me to the terminal, I missed my flight. As a result, I also missed my son's high school graduation ceremony. This is something neither he nor I ever will forget. It is an event, of course, that cannot be duplicated in my life.

I am quite bitter about your lapse of service. But I will, for the moment, continue to use your cars because you are conveniently located.

ACTION INTENDED

I trust that the slow service to which I refer was a rare event. If it happens again, I will inform the travel director of my company.

Yours truly,

RESTAURANT: UNJUSTIFIED DELAY IN SEATING

November 25, 19__

Mr. Roger Clever, Manager
Roger's Food Palace
11-11 Wegotcha Lane
Cleveland, OH 92999

Dear Mr. Clever:

POSITIVE STATEMENT You operate a very clean restaurant with a pleasant, relaxing environment. But I have a complaint.

COMPLAINT HISTORY Our party of six waited 50 minutes past the reservation time last Friday evening. Your maitre d' suggested that we wait in the lounge.

SUPPORTING FACTS You know that you could have seated us earlier, probably at the reservation time. When we were shown to our seat we saw three empty tables.

ACTION REQUESTED I suggest that you begin seating your customers at the time for which they make reservations. I promise you that my friends and myself will spread word of your poor service as widely as we can, and encourage our friends to do the same, unless you change your policy.

Sincerely,

SOFT GOODS STORE: POOR SERVICE

November 13, 19__

Mr. Peter Warroad, President
Wonderful, Inc.
36 Marvelous Dr.
Heavenly, OH 66778

Dear Mr. Warroad:

POSITIVE STATEMENT/ PROBLEM

I wish to thank you for years of good service.

However, your record is not intact, considering that you have refused to credit my account for a coat that I wish to return because of obviously inferior workmanship.

COMPLAINT HISTORY

I purchased the coat in September. The first time I wore it, I reached for my car door and the sleeve nearly ripped off at the shoulder seam.

Your salesperson, Harold Wainright, refused to accept the coat in return. He insisted upon exchanging it. But, frankly, I am so disgusted with the terrible quality of the coat that I don't want to take a chance on another coat from you.

I'll most likely continue to buy dresses and accessories from you, however.

ACTION REQUESTED

I will return the coat; and I want the $250 cost of the coat plus tax credited to my account, number 918273. Also, please remove finance charges of $13 from my billing.

Sincerely,

STATE GOVERNMENT COMPLAINT

January 2, 19__

Mr. Hugh Hufnagel
Director, Motor Vehicle Services Division
State of Anxiety
Normal, IL 55555

Dear Mr. Hufnagel:

POSITIVE OPENING

You, Mr. Hufnagel, are a public official. That means to me that you are sensitive to the needs and opinions of the public.

COMPLAINT HISTORY

I have a strong opinion about the bad attitudes and the rotten service by clerks in the motor vehicle department facility on Failsafe Street.

SUPPORTING FACTS

Let me give you the facts. On December 30, I sat in your spacious lobby on one of your backless stools for 62 minutes before my number was called. After that I waited in line for another 40 minutes. Just as I reached the head of the line the clerk triumphantly and with a flourish slid her little rectangular message board in front of me. "CLOSED" it read. And she was gone, leaving me to stand there feeling stupid and then enraged.

EXPANSION OF COMPLAINT

Now, I ask you as a politically sensitive position, is this any way to treat a constituent? I doubt that I am the only person that this has ever happened to. Now consider that I will be very vocal in discussing this matter with my state legislator and with friends and relatives.

ACTION REQUESTED

Please forcefully impress upon your clerks the revolutionary idea that *citizens are people*!

Sincerely,

TELEVISION STATION: MISLEADING ADVERTISING

January 19, 19__

Mr. John Smith
General Sales Manager, WXYZ-TV
Farmington, MO 10101

Dear Mr. Smith:

COMPLAINT

I would like to know why your TV station allowed the blatantly misleading commercial for BBB Midtown Hotel in New York to air last night, twice, during your Sunday night movie.

I can personally attest to the fact that BBB Midtown Hotel offers neither friendly nor efficient service. I stayed there several times, and I know.

ACTION REQUESTED

There wasn't an ounce of truth in the commercial and I would like to know when it's going to be pulled from the air and why you allowed it to be run in the first place.

Sincerely,

BUILDING CONTRACTOR: WORKMANSHIP

February 23, 19__

Mr. Harry Stringer, President
Stringer Construction Co.
Webuildem, MU 11229

Dear Mr. Stringer:

POSITIVE STATEMENT

Although you worked very fast and cleaned up the debris resulting from your work in building my attached garage, I have a complaint. The overhead door cannot be opened.

BUSINESS BENEFIT

I have talked with your foreman twice. But my last conversation was nearly two weeks ago. At that time he promised to correct the garage door problem "in two days."

I'm sure that you want to correct any problem resulting from poor workmanship to avoid developing a bad reputation in the community.

ACTION REQUESTED

So, please open my door and do whatever must be done to make sure that I will be able to open and close it in the future.

PLEASANT REQUEST FOR RESPONSE

Will you please call and tell me when you'll be out to open the door? My phone number is: 461-2859.

Sincerely,

CHAPTER 14
COMPLAINING IN PERSON

"Speak softly...but carry a big stick."

— ADVOCATED BY PRESIDENT TEDDY ROOSEVELT

You've done it. Your letters and phone calls have paid off and you're going in for a face-to-face talk with a supervisor, a manager, the customer service manager, or (you can't believe it) with a corporate vice president or president.

Of course, you tried talking to the employee who snubbed you or misinformed you, to that person's superior, and to the customer service department. None of that helped.

You're going to tell the executive why your complaint is justified; and you're going to ask for satisfaction.

Prepare: Reduce the stress of a personal meeting with an executive focusing upon you from behind a huge desk. Do it by "role playing."

A friend sits behind a desk or a table looking stern and unresponsive. Imagine that your friend really is the executive you are to meet. (No giggling, now.) Tell her or him about your problem and what you expect the executive to do about it.

If you role play, we guarantee you that you'll feel more in control of the situation when you face the real executive. You won't be as nervous as you would have been without practicing for the meeting.

Role playing isn't for everyone; but, if *you* happen to be very determined to right a wrong, you'll see the wisdom in this idea.

Dress well. No jeans or baggy or rumpled clothing. Hair must be clean, neatly cut, and styled. Your statements will carry more weight if you *look* reliable and decisive than they will if you look as if you were homeless.

It helps if you take someone with you, even *several* friends and neighbors, all of them customers or at least potential customers. There definitely *is* strength in numbers in this situation. An office full of unhappy customers very likely will kindle visions of declining sales and even spontaneous boycott in the mind of the executive.

Speak softly...but, as President Teddy Roosevelt advocated, carry a big stick. Be firm. Be persistent. And don't back down.

If you yell, wave your arms, and make threats that you couldn't keep, you will win only the executive's determination to deny your request.

Don't ever give the impression that you are embarrassed, unsure of your facts, or having difficulty expressing yourself. Instead, imply that you are *accustomed* to getting satisfaction when you complain. State that you're not going to stop complaining until you *do* get satisfaction.

You might say that you have a busy schedule and that you expect the matter to be settled then and there.

Even if you're getting no response, *keep talking*. Use the broken record technique: Repeat your main point. After you've said the same thing in six or seven different ways, the manager, supervisor, or vice president probably will conclude that giving you what you want is a lot easier than arguing with you.

Sometime during a meeting ask, if necessary: "What would *you* do if you were in my shoes?" Imply that it's logical and fair for you to request redress for your service problem.

To win the executive's cooperation, say something like: "I'm in business, too, and I would be upset to learn that one of my company's customers was treated as poorly as I've been treated."

As a last resort, exert a powerful impact by telling the company that it might as well "kiss off" both *your* repeat business and that of your friends and neighbors. Remember, companies depend upon repeat customers for most of their business.

The recapitulation: If you complain assertively and if you are persistent, there's a good chance that you'll get the satisfaction that you deserve.

Chapter 15

BETTER BUSINESS BUREAUS

"Better Business Bureaus are so convenient that they are worth special comment."

Better Business Bureaus are so convenient (there's probably an office near you) that they are worth special comment.

A Better Business Bureau (BBB) performs two basic functions:

1. maintaining files on companies and
2. handling gripes.

BBBs represent manufacturers and retailers and are funded by them.

Files consist mainly of logs of public inquiries and complaints. But, unless a complainant names a company, no file will be available.

Always lodge legitimate complaints with the local BBB office to help them update their files and improve their service. By doing so you are doing a favor for other consumers.

When a local bureau gets enough complaints on a company, it "profiles" the concern. The profile includes the company's record in handling consumer complaints. And it details lawsuits that have been filed against the company. Profiles and other file information is available to consumers without charge.

If you've been ripped off, fill out a BBB Customer Experience Record (CER) form.

Filing a complaint with your local Better Business Bureau yields the same results, generally, as going to self-regulatory bodies set up by companies in the same business. The BBB works closely with business.

Don't expect legal help from the BBB. They won't get involved in law suits.

The bureau will send your CER form to the company and ask for an answer. That's all. The company can answer it and settle the dispute, offer its own version of the dispute, or ignore the form.

BBBs have no enforcement powers. Their strength comes merely from its records of complaints that are shared with consumers.

A BBB can provide leverage when you deal with an out-of-state firm. This is important because some firms move very slowly or not at all when dealing with people who live in distant states. They know that you are unlikely to show up on their doorsteps.

If you have genuine differences with a BBB member company, the BBB will conduct arbitration in many states. But, both parties must agree to arbitration.

An attorney is not needed. The outcome — the arbitrator's decision — usually is legally binding in a court of law.

Don't place all your faith in your local BBB, though. Some are tougher than others. Some are strongly influenced by their business members.

While the BBB claims that 77.5 percent of all complaints are "settled," that doesn't mean the consumer is always satisfied. The BBB counts any "reasonable" offer by a company *or* rejection of an "unjustified claim" as a "settlement."

Look in the phone book for the bureau nearest you. Or write: Council of Better Business Bureaus, Inc., 1150 Seventeenth St. NW, Washington, DC 20036, 202-862-1200.

CHAPTER 16

LOCAL MEDIA ACTION LINES

"The court of last resort."

For some consumers, the media are their "court of last resort." But, others look upon the media as their court of *first* resort.

Many newspapers and radio and TV stations, but not all of them, maintain consumer help services often called "Action Line" services. They attempt to resolve problems and publish or air reports on their efforts and results.

About 134 daily newspapers in 130 different cities and 39 states have "reader service" editors, at last report.

The *New York Daily News* receives 2500 consumer complaints a week. The paper responds by writing to each "offender" that a consumer complains about. Twenty complaints a day are published in the paper with an account of how the complaints were resolved.

Similar services exist at many radio and TV stations in the U.S., such as WCCO-TV in Minneapolis-St. Paul. The station receives viewer tips to widespread abuses and then produces special programs to address them.

Becoming "Villain of the Day" on the local TV station is a frightening and motivating prospect for businesspeople. That's why threatening to contact "Action Line" is a very good way to elevate recalcitrant businesspeople from their chairs.

But, you must present your case in a way that excites reading and viewing audiences. The media like action stories involving named people and places that produce excitingly visual TV coverage or riveting newspaper copy.

When you cite *specific cases* in which you were insulted, treated rudely, or ignored by a business, you have a good chance of seeing your complaint in print.

As for political appointees to government jobs, they all know that there are legions of reporters out there itching for a chance to barbecue the bureaucrats over the fires of public indignation. Newspaper and electronic media consumer services are an effective way to jar politicians and bureaucrats out of their apathy, brought on by the fact that they have the only show in town: They have no competitors. Some of them are experts at the take-it-or-leave-it game.

If there's one thing a politician can't stand, it's adverse exposure in the mass media. They all want to be admired and flattered in the press.

To find the names of stations, newspapers, and their personnel who staff these consumer services, call your city or state consumer affairs office. It's usually listed in the white pages of the telephone book under the name of your city or state.

CHAPTER 17

COMPANY HOT LINES

"Many manufacturers of consumer products maintain free '800' exchange numbers."

Whirlpool Corporation's Cool-Line service (1-800-253-1301 in most states) devotes most of its resources to answering the question: "Where can I find service for my appliance?"

Cool-Line pioneered hot line service when it began in 1967, answering consumer questions.

General Electric started a similar service in the mid-1980s. Called the General Electric Answer Center (1-800-626-2000), more than three million calls were handled in 1988.

GE's is a sophisticated operation. Consumers benefit because the system incorporates built-in incentives for dealers to provide good service locally.

The Answer Center refers consumers to the dealer in their neighborhoods because many consumer inquiries and complaints (some 800,000 of them in a recent year) can be dealt with best by local dealers. In effect, then, the Answer Center is referring potential new customers to local dealers. (That's smart.)

But, and here's the twist, dealers that are in GE's "little black book" of dealers with unsatisfactory service ratings do not receive referrals. That's bad because many referrals lead to sales, and dealers know it. So, GE dealers tend to work hard to provide good service.

A textbook case history in bottom-line benefits of customer service has been written by the performance of Proctor & Gamble (P&G), the nation's largest producer of consumer products. P&G prints an "800" number — 1-800-543-0485 — on all of its products. Other companies also print "800" numbers on their products or merchandise.

During the latest annual reporting period, P&G reported answering about a million telephone calls and letters from customers, according to Dorothy Puccini, Manager of Consumer Services.

A third of these replies deal with gripes about products, complaints about ads, and even with plots of TV soap operas sponsored by the company.

Many manufacturers of consumer products maintain free "800" exchange numbers. More than 750 corporate complaint lines are listed in the *Consumer's Resource Handbook*; most of them are toll-free. Obtain a free copy of the handbook from: Consumer Information Center, Dept. 78, Pueblo, CO 81009.

The Great 800 Directory also lists "800" numbers of manufacturers and of government agencies. It is published by The Great 800 Directory Co., P.O. Box 6944, Jackson, MS 39212. The book is available in most larger libraries. The directory provides the means to call up many companies and, at no charge to you, talk to a real, live person.

Here are a few often-used "800" numbers from *The Great 800 Directory*:

- ❑ Consumer Product Safety Commission: 1-800-638-2772.
- ❑ Insurance Information Institute's Consumer Hot Line: 1-800-821-0477.
- ❑ MACAP — Major Appliance Consumer Action Panel: 1-800-621-0477.

Your library may have another directory that will give you the address and phone number of the company you wish to contact if it doesn't have *The Great 800 Directory*. Just ask.

Standard and Poor's Register and *Consumers' Index to Product Evaluations and Information Sources*, found in most libraries, also provide name, address, and phone number information. *Standard and Poor's* lists the names of presidents and other corporate officers.

You can also call the telephone company's toll-free information number (1-800-555-1212) to find out the "800" number of a company you wish to call.

Employees staffing hot lines are trained to know policy and procedures and to tell you what to do and whom to contact.

If you have lost all the paper that accompanied a purchase and if a product does not carry an address or phone number, call the Better Business Bureau. The BBB maintains a list of many manufacturers.

But, if you still can't find information needed to contact retail or manufacturing companies, you might be able to obtain it from either of two membership groups for customer service professionals:

SOCIETY OF CONSUMER AFFAIRS PROFESSIONALS IN BUSINESS (SOCAP)
801 North Fairfax Street, 4th Floor
Alexandria, VA 22314
703-519-3700

INTERNATIONAL CUSTOMER SERVICE ASSN. (ICSA)
401 North Michigan Avenue
Chicago, IL 60611
312-321-6800

The memberships of these two organizations represent most of the top 1,000 businesses in the United States.

CHAPTER 18

SUE THE BUMS

"I did it! I did it!"

If all else fails in your attempt to get satisfaction in a serious and flagrant case of consumer abuse by any type of business, file a law suit.

Sue in Small Claims Court where the average award is about $500. Or, for a higher claim, sue in District Court. By the way, use of an attorney is not necessary in Small Claims Court but is advisable in District Court.

Before you bring suit, though, write a "demand letter" — a demand for the satisfaction that you desire. You may get a surprise in the mail — an unexpected settlement or a satisfactory counteroffer.

Then you can run out the door, waving your arms and yelling for all the neighbors to hear: "I did it! I did it!"

ARBITRATION

If you can't get satisfaction working on your own, consider arbitration. Start with a Better Business Bureau or the American Arbitration Association (AAA), 140 W. 51st St., New York, NY 10020. Phone: 212-484-4000. The American Arbitration Association maintains a Community Dispute Service and is the largest of a dozen or so independent arbitration organizations. AAA maintains 32 regional offices.

Arbitration is a fast, inexpensive, and legally binding means of settling claims outside of court. Both parties (that includes you) pay an administration fee.

Arbitration is especially useful in problems with contractors related to remodeling and building and in computer disputes and insurance claims.

Arbitration doesn't come cheaply, though. According to the American Arbitration Association, cases involving up to $20,000 require an administrative fee of 3 percent of the amount being sought — a minimum of $300.

Business owners must agree to an AAA hearing. It is in their best interests to do so to avoid expensive, drawn-out court hearings.

Some companies, such as Chrysler Corporation, have their own arbitration boards.

CHAPTER 19

GET HELP

"Knowledge is power."

Directories
Industry Panels
Allies
Federal AgenciesBooks
Magazine and Newspaper Articles

When a business refuses to correct a problem, we must ask for help from consumer groups and government agencies.

If you know whom to contact and how to go about complaining, you have an advantage over consumers who either don't know how to proceed with a complaint or who follow the grin-and-bear-it philosophy of life. Knowledge is power.

Organizations listed in this chapter can give you *specific* contact and procedure information and assistance that often spells the difference between futility and success.

Most of these organizations will want to know what you've done already to solve a problem — letters you've sent, phone calls you've made, and so on. So, do everything you can think of — everything that you can be expected to do as an individual.

Keep careful records of every move you make and the responses you receive.

Remember that groups set up to help you gain your rights won't enter the fray until you've exhausted normal recourses. They expect to see documented proof of unsuccessful efforts to resolve the problem on your own.

One of the most helpful organizations is Consumer Federation of America, 1012 14th Street NW, Washington, DC 20005.

The Useful Almanac, an annual publication of Consumer News, Inc., Washington, DC 20045, provides virtually all the information that a consumer needs to pursue satisfaction. Consumer News also publishes *Directory of State and Local Consumer Groups*.

The *Consumer's Resource Handbook* is available, free, from the Consumer Information Center, Dept. 78, Pueblo, CO 81009.

You may need to find a telephone number, preferably a toll-free number. One of the best "800" directories is *Toll-Free Digest*. The latest issue contains more than 43,000 toll-free telephone numbers. You can create a lot of havoc with this many free calls. A recent cost, that may have increased by now, is $17.95. (*Toll-Free Digest*, Box 800, Claverac, NY 12513, 518-828-6400 or 1-800-447-4700. In Illinois: 1-800-322-4400. You can use MasterCard or Visa to pay for it.

In the *Toll-Free Digest* you will find the following under "Business Associations":

NATIONAL ACADEMY OF CONCILIATORS
1-800-638-8242

NATIONAL RESTAURANT ASSOCIATION
1-800-424-5156

U.S. CHAMBER OF COMMERCE
1-800-424-6746.

Another "800" directory is *The Great 800 Toll-Free Directory*, P.O. Box 6944, Jackson, MS 39212. Contact them at 1-800-626-1033 except in Mississippi, where the number is 601-944-0123. They call themselves "the nation's largest, most complete "800" telephone directory." It covers the United States, Puerto Rico, and the Virgin Islands.

This directory is arranged alphabetically and contains an alphabetical index.

The *National Directory* of addresses and telephone numbers is published by General Information, Inc., 401 Parkplace, Suite 305, Kirkland, WA 98033. Phone: 206-828-4777. The latest information is that this directory costs $45 plus $4.50 mailing charge. Send check or money order, or use your Visa, MasterCard, or American Express credit card. Corporations are listed alphabetically (52,000 of them) and by industry classification. *The AT&T Toll-Free "800" Directory* costs $14.95. Call your phone company's business office to order it.

Find Federal government agencies and departments in the *U.S. Government Manual*, publication number 022-003-00948-5. Cost: $6.50 from U.S. Government Printing Office, Superintendent of Documents, Washington, DC 20242.

Find names, addresses, and phone numbers of senators and congressmen who sit on committees that oversee the agency you're arguing with in the *Congressional Directory*, available for $6.50 from the Government Printing Office. When contacting your congressman or senator, write to the staff director of each committee and *also* to each committee member.

INDUSTRY PANELS

To improve customer relations, many industries have created self-regulating panels to handle consumer complaints. These panels review details of a complaint and offer suggestions on how the problem can be resolved. Here are some of them:

AMERICAN SOCIETY OF TRAVEL AGENTS
4400 MacArthur Blvd. NW
Washington, DC 20007
703-739-2782

AUTOCAP—AUTOMOTIVE CONSUMER ACTION PROGRAM
8400 Westpark Dr.
McLean, VA 22102
703-821-7000

DIRECT MAIL/MARKETING ASSOCIATION
Mail Order Action Line
6 E. 43 St.
New York, NY 10017
212-689-4977

DIRECT SELLING ASSOCIATION
(Door-to-Door Sales)
Director of Consumer Affairs
1730 M St. NW, Suite 610
Washington, DC 20036
202-293-5760

ELECTRONIC INDUSTRIES ASSOCIATION.
Office of Consumer Affairs
2001 I St. NW
Washington, DC 10006
202-457-4900

FICAP — FURNITURE INDUSTRY CONSUMER
ACTION PANEL
P.O. Box HP7
High Point, NC 27261
919-884-5000

(ICAP) INSURANCE CONSUMER ACTION PANEL
640 Investment Building
Washington, DC 20005
202-628-1300

INTERNATIONAL FABRICARE INSTITUTE
(Dry Cleaners)
12251 Tech Road
Silver Spring, MD 20904
301-622-1900

JEWELERS VIGILANCE COMMITTEE
919 Third Av.
New York, NY 10022
212-753-1304

MACAP—MAJOR APPLIANCE CONSUMER ACTION PANEL
20 North Wacker Dr.
Chicago, IL 60606
1-800-621-0477

NATIONAL ASSOCIATION OF STATE UTILITY
CONSUMER ADVOCATES
c/o Florida Public Counsel
Crown Bldg.
202 Blount St., Rm. 624
Tallahassee, FL 32301
904-488-9330

NATIONAL INSTITUTE FOR AUTOMOTIVE SERVICE
EXCELLENCE
202-833-9646

To find the names of certified auto repair shops in your area, you can also contact the local office of the American Automobile Association.

PHOTO MARKETING ASSOCIATION
3000 Picture Place
Jackson, MI 49201
517-788-8100

THANACAP—FUNERAL SERVICE CONSUMER ACTION PANEL
11121 W. Oklahoma Av.
Milwaukee, WI 53227
404-541-7925

TIRE DEALERS AND RETREADERS ASSOCIATION
Field Operations Department
1343 L St. NW
Washington, DC 20005
202-638-6650
Indiana: 317-631-8124
Wisconsin: 414-774-6590

Here are a few contacts for financial institution matters:

NATIONAL BANKS
Comptroller of the Currency
Director of Consumer Activities
Department of the Treasury
490 L'Enfant Plaza SW
Washington, DC 20219
202-287-4265.

STATE BANKS & TRUST COMPANIES
Board of Governors of the Federal Reserve System
Division of Consumer and Community Affairs
Washington, DC 20551
202-452-3946

ALL OTHER BANKS
Federal Deposit Insurance Corporation
Office of Consumer Affairs
550 17th Street NW (F130)
Washington, DC 20429

CREDIT BUREAUS
Federal Trade Commission (FTC)
Division of Credit Practices
6th and Pennsylvania Av. NW
Washington, DC 20580.

The FTC keeps complaints on file. If a file grows large they investigate. Regional FTC offices are listed in the government pages of the telephone book. Or, request specific information about the Equal Credit Opportunity Act, Truth-In-Lending Act, Fair Credit Billing Act, and Fair Debt Collection Practices Act.

CREDIT CARDS
Bankcard Holders of America
560 Herndon Parkway, Suite 120,
Herndon, VA 22070
703-481-1110.

Educational publications designed to help you manage and save money and solve your credit problems. Discloses features of the Fair Credit and Charge Card Disclosure Act.

SAVINGS AND LOAN ASSOCIATIONS; SAVINGS BANKS
Office of Thrift Supervision
Consumer Affairs
1700 G St. NW
Washington, DC 20552

ALLIES

Find "allies" — collaborators — in your search for problem resolution. A hotel concierge is the classic example of a powerful ally. Many airlines have "flight-service directors" or "passenger-service agents" charged with resolving passenger problems on the spot.

More than 60 percent of hospitals in the United States have "patient advocates." They intervene for patients when meals are served cold or when they feel they've been brushed off by a doctor.

Many department stores have personal shoppers who call around to find a preferred size or color.

FEDERAL AGENCIES

For a free guide listing federal agencies *and* local corporate consumer contacts, write for the *Consumer's Resource Handbook*, Consumer Information Center, Dept. 78, Pueblo, CO 81009.

These are some of the entries in the Handbook:

CONSUMER PRODUCT SAFETY COMMISSION
Office of Public Affairs
Washington, DC 20207
1-800-638-2772

FEDERAL TRADE COMMISSION
Correspondence Branch
6th St. & Pennsylvania Av. NW
Washington, DC 20580
202-326-3128

Also in the *Consumer's Resource Handbook* is contact information for:

- ❑ U.S. Postal Service
- ❑ U.S. Dept. of Health & Human Services
- ❑ Consumer Information Center of the General Services
- ❑ Administration
- ❑ United States Office of Consumer Affairs.

BOOKS

These reference books for consumers can be purchased through book stores. Many libraries have them, too.

You Can Negotiate Anything, by Herb Cohen.

The Art of Negotiating, by Herb Nierenberg.

Getting People to Say Yes, by Stephen Pollan.

Reader's Digest Consumer Advisor. An Action Guide. Reader's Digest Assn., Inc. Lists state attorneys general offices, BBB offices by state; and state offices of consumer affairs.

Fighting Back, by Dana Shilling. Contains sample consumer complaint letters for every imaginable situation: Services, utilities, landlords, credit and banking, media, and government.

Consumer Source Book, by Gale Research Co., Detroit. Lists consumer organizations at every level of government and virtually every private consumer group.

Satisfaction Guaranteed: The Ultimate Guide to Consumer

Satisfaction Guaranteed: The Ultimate Guide to Consumer Self Defense, Linden Press/Simon & Schuster.

Quality Customer Service, by William B. Martin.

Getting What You Deserve, by Stephen A. Newman and Nancy Kramer.

Fight Back!, by David Horowitz.

Consumer Revenge, by Christopher Gilson, Linda Cawley, and Rick Schmidt. G.P. Putnam's Sons.

Get Even: The Complete Book of Dirty Tricks, by George Hayduke, Paladin Press.

MAGAZINE AND NEWSPAPER ARTICLES

Magazines and newspapers often contain very useful articles. The media named here can be found in large or medium-size libraries. Or, you can write to the magazine publishers (Circulation Dept.) or newspapers (Library or Circulation Dept.) and ask for copies. You will be charged.

1. *Fortune*, "What Sam Walton taught America," by Bill Saporito. May 4, 1992.

2. *Ladies Home Journal*, "How to Use Consumer Clout," by Melanie Berger. March 1992. ABSTRACT: Complaining about a product or service that doesn't measure up will often get results. The various steps of the complaint process described. Always start with the merchant who sold you the product.

3. *Mpls.-St. Paul Magazine*, "Wresting the Best From a Restaurant," by Carla Waldemar. March 1992. ABSTRACT: Tips on getting good service at a restaurant include communicating with the server, asking questions about the menu, tipping appropriately, and letting the staff know in advance if it is a special occasion. A list of pointers from a restaurateur is included.

4. *Kiplinger's Personal Finance Magazine*, "How to Get the Service You Deserve," by Kristin Davis. February 1992. ABSTRACT: Tips on getting quality service are provided.

5. *PC-Computing*, "Shoddy Service? Don't Get Mad, Fight Back!" by Wendy Taylor. March 1991.

6. *Consumers' Research Magazine*, "How to Handle Your Own Complaint," July 1989.

7. *Flower & Garden Magazine*, "How to be a Good Service Customer," by Doc Sprockett. April 1989.

8. *Money*, "Best ways to get your money back," by Sylvia Nasar. April, 1989. State-by-state guide to small claimscourt.

9. *Consumers Digest*, March-April 1987, "Guide to Washington Consumer Advocacy Groups." Includes Federal Agencies.

10. *Washingtonian*, February 1986, "How to Get Help: A Directory of Where to Complain."

11. *Washingtonian*, February 1986, "When bad service turns you into a wimp, try these sure-fire strategies."

12. *Consumers Digest*, November-December 1984, "What Drives Us Nuts: How to Survive in Today's Supermarket."

CHAPTER 20

YOUR OWN CONSUMER GROUP

"You still can fight City Hall and win."

Sometimes, after you've been forced to escalate your complaint to consumer organizations and government consumer agencies, you'll find that it's difficult to find someone who's willing to act on your complaint when it is a *service* complaint.

If a product doesn't work or it's dangerous, if you don't get what you pay for, if a product breaks within a warranty period, if a shyster bilks you, or even if advertised claims are misleading, there are plenty of agencies, departments, offices, bureaus and commissions to help you get redress for the wrongs visited upon you.

Plenty of organizations fight for safety. For quality. For non-polluting products. For products that don't violate this law or that.

But, virtually no organizations fight for *service*. Few organizations fight against rudeness, ignorance, and companies prowling in the shadows of legitimate business enterprise by promising and reneging, misleading and price-gouging.

This should encourage you to start your own organization. Remember that bad service is one area in which personal initiative still is effective: You still can fight City Hall and win.

Perhaps the absence of groups that help consumers resolve poor-service complaints will encourage you to form your own consumer group.

There is strength in numbers. Look for friends or acquaintances who are as disgusted as you with service by a particular business or industry. Then, complain... each of you, independently. You'll create a very loud noise that your target business certainly will hear.

Even two people complaining have a greater impact than one lone voice of complaint. A single dissenter could be just a whiner having a bad day, a businessowner might reason. A manager might be able to rationalize away your complaint by saying to himself/herself: "Aw, this customer just got up on the wrong side of the bed this morning."

But, two or three or four complainers together, or a delegation that represents a group of hundreds...that's a bad sign, for sure.

Before beginning to organize your own consumer group, check around to see if a group with the same general objectives as yours already exists. It would be easier for you to start with an existing organization, unless it's a group with a bad image, than it is to build a group from scratch.

Furthermore, if other people in your community have organized into a group to fight issues similar to your issues, carefully consider joining the existing group instead of starting another one. It's better to enlist their help and to tap their experience and good will than to arouse their jealousy by forming another group.

To find such groups, check local newspapers and interview reporters who've covered consumer issues. Check with local government agencies and the largest church and social service organizations.

Also, go to your local library and check:

Directory of State and Local Consumer Groups, published by Consumer Federation of America, 1012 14th St. NW, Washington, DC 20005.

HELP: The Useful Almanac, which is an annual publication of Consumer News, Inc., Washington, DC 20045.

A city or county consumer protection office can tell you the names and give you the contact information for existing local consumer groups.

The consumer protection office can be found under the name of the city or county in the phone book. Call the office and obtain their mailing address.

State consumer protection offices are listed in the phone book, under the name of the state.

If you can't find the phone number of the city, county or state consumer protection office, get help by calling the general number for your city or state government offices.

Now, let's say that you've learned that there are no consumer groups in your area with substantially the same objectives as you. You're ready to begin forming your own group. Here's how to proceed:

1. Visit any remotely similar groups within about a radius to find out how they are organized, how they started, and what their most effective tactics are.

2. Hold an organizational meeting as soon as you have several people interested in participating, not just "joining." Set an agenda. Don't dominate the meeting: Let others add agenda items and make suggestions.

3. Decide on the type of activity you want to pursue first. Don't dissipate your energies by tackling too many things at once.

4. Assign specific tasks to people in line with their experience, abilities, and willingness to work. Share responsibility and any glory: It's a mistake for the whole operation to depend upon one person.

5. Set small, reachable goals. Achieve quantifiable goals as soon as possible. Achievement motivates.

6. Don't be concerned about raising money, at first. Fund-raising is time consuming. Raising money is easier after you have a couple of concrete accomplishments to point to as reasons why people should contribute. Meet in someone's home and chip in or share cost of phoning, supplies, and transportation. Sharing can bind a group together.

Meet with a few neighbors and friends to get started. Give your organization a name. Perhaps buy buttons that say SOS (Save Our Service) or something else that you like.

Then target the worst service and go see the manager of the business. When he or she learns that you represent a *group*, you'll get much better results than you would as an individual.

Your consumer group needn't be a separate organization, remember. You can set it up as sort of a committee of your existing Neighborhood Association — or service club, employee association, union, or precinct or ward political organization.

CHAPTER 21

GET TOUGH: GUERILLA TACTICS

"When the going gets tough,
the tough get going."

— NATIONAL ADVERTISER

There's value in that adage. Getting "tough" is what a consumer must do when all legitimate, ordinary methods of achieving satisfaction have been rebuffed by hardnosed business people.

But: Don't interpret "getting tough" as "getting *mean.*"

Don't use an innocent employee as a whipping post.

Don't say nasty things to salespeople as an emotional release.

In other words, bend over backward to avoid being *unreasonable.*

You can find justification for a charitable attitude toward business, government departments, or non-profit organizations in a little test. Point out dissatisfaction (instead of letting dissatisfaction seethe and bubble within you) to five different businesses and take note of their responses.

You'll probably leave each place of business — or, at least, four out of five — either with a smile on your face or warmth in your heart. The businesses will have hurried to correct your problem.

By "complaining" you will illustrate the spirit of this book for yourself. Businesses, government departments, and non-profit organizations concerned with quality service usually correct faults when they know about them. In most instances faults that go *un*corrected are those that neither employees nor customers told managers about.

Of course, exceptions exist. Some business people who are very aware of the service dissatisfactions of their customers still spend nothing for a service system. However, they may spend a great deal on new buildings, on a new fleet of delivery trucks, or on store remodeling, fancy merchandise displays, and full-page ads that tout their "Personal Service With a Smile."

It's classic head-in-the-sand behavior. The problem of bad service clearly exists. Many studies prove it. Yet, some businesspeople resist correcting bad service to the death — their businesses' death.

Some businesses seem to get by for years on skinflint service. (They certainly don't develop a large following of loyal customers that way, however.) They provide service that's just barely good enough to hold enough customers to keep them in business.

But, they certainly leave themselves vulnerable to downturns in the economy, to new competition, and to demographic changes.

Eventually, many of them disappear from the economic scene.

Then we don't have to worry about their bad service anymore.

Now that we are committed to decency and fair play, even for businesspeople who deliberately ignore customers and overlook the bad service that they provide, here are some effective "get tough" tactics — "guerilla tactics."

THE MUG SHOT

The Get Tough consumer carries a Polaroid camera. If a salesperson gives bad service, pull it out, snap a picture of the employee, and say: "I need a picture to send in with my complaint."

What you're really after is service then and there. You want the employee's attention so you can point out a problem.

A micro-size tape recorder can record a surly clerk's actual words and convict him "out of his own mouth," if you decide that service was bad enough to warrant a visit to his or her supervisor.

THE BROKEN RECORD

Another successful technique was developed by specialists in assertiveness training. It's called "The Broken Record."

There you are in the camera department. Business is brisk and, obviously, your salesperson is overly eager to be finished with you.

You ask: "Does this camera have an automatic focus? How does it work?"

The salesman answers: "Most cameras made by this manufacturer do."

He responds with a similar curt comment every time you repeat the question.

But, you are persistent. You *continue* to ask the question over and over again. You change the words... sure. But, basically, you ask the same question until you get a specific answer — *no matter what the serviceperson says in response.*

Sometimes, a stubborn salesperson finally will answer. But, be alert for people who fabricate answers that sound good but are total fiction, just to get rid of you.

TIT FOR TAT

Here's a counterattack to use against complaint handlers trained to "depersonalize" callers by instantly asking for account numbers even before saying hello. They may even interrupt your opening sentence to say in a crisp, efficient voice: "May I have your account number, puh-leeze?"

So, do the same thing. After you give such a person your account number say: "Now, please give me your name and employee number."

Write down the person's name. Also write down the promises the customer service representative makes — or note the fact that the complaint handler makes no promises at all.

THE OLD "LOUD VOICE TECHNIQUE"

Perhaps you can use this idea: Raise the volume of your voice. Say loudly but not angrily: "I'm not moving until you straighten this out!"

Other customers become uneasy and they quickly evacuate the area to avoid the unpleasant scene. A smart employee or supervisor does almost *anything* to satisfy you and get rid of you.

Arlene Cantlon of Riverdale, Illinois, really did lose her temper in a discount outlet because the store was making a habit, in her opinion, of failing to have advertised goods in stock.

"I asked to speak to the salesgirl in the shoe department, but nobody knew where she was. I waited 35 minutes while they looked for her. Nobody could find her, so I asked to see the store manager.

"At this point I had a crowd of customers cheering me on. One woman said to me, 'It won't do any good, but go for it!'"

Cantlon finally got her audience with the manager and some of the merchandise she wanted as well.

It was a notable victory; and it need not be rare. Follow Arlene Cantlon's example and you will get satisfaction.

One irate customer caused a half-hour shutdown of a department in a major retail store. The customer had ordered a product and received the wrong item; so he returned it. Again he received the wrong item; and again he returned it.

He ended up receiving the wrong item eleven times in a row and returning it eleven times. He was heard on the floor below shouting at a clerk: "This is the *eleventh* time."

When last seen he was loudly offering to fight the security men dragging him away.

What this customer did wrong was to become visibly and vocally angry. Anger is a sure way to *not* get what you want. Instead, allow yourself...yes, even encourage yourself...to become "indignant." That's civilized anger. The dictionary calls indignation "anger aroused by something unjust."

COMMUNICATE: JUST THE FACTS, MA'AM

Sometimes all you need to do is present your case to a person who has authority to make decisions.

A housewife reported that the service contract on her family's personal computer expired before a renewal of the contract had been offered by the retailer. Although only six days had elapsed, a salesman insisted that the equipment had to be inspected at the store (for $25) or at home ($100) before another contract could be issued.

But, when the housewife phoned the manager, he waived the rules and renewed — without inspection.

PROPAGANDA CAMPAIGN

If you are committed to buying at a place near your home because it is much closer than any other business of its kind, you have a stake in good service. This nearby business may think that "service" is mere "maintenance" — fixing your lawn mower, for instance.

Clearly, it's best when the consumer confronts businesses with their complaints. But for people who are really uncomfortable expressing their complaints verbally — who would instead simply leave and not ever come back — there is another way to pursue the problem.

For those people a long-term propaganda campaign may be just the ticket.

Have your neighborhood fast-print shop print inexpensive cards that you distribute in the store — and in other stores. They bear pointed messages such as:

"I hope you enjoyed your chat. I didn't." (Service employees sometimes keep customers waiting while they hash over last night's party or yesterday's game.)

"Forgive me for imposing on your time."

"Quick! Give me one good reason why you should take out your bad mood on me."

"I don't have to come here to get insulted. I can get insulted at home."

"Please accept my sincerest apologies for having the *nerve* to ask you a question about the product/service that you sell."

"Your Ignorance (Of the Products You Sell) Is Not *My* Bliss."

Spot the cards in conspicuous places as close as possible to the point where poor service occurred.

After noticing the cards over a period of days, managers and supervisors might get the point: They have a dissatisfied customer or maybe even a lot of dissatisfied customers.

You can't help it, can you, if your activity gives the impression that a group of people are "carding" the store? You are just a modern-day Johnny Appleseed serving society.

Your print shop can set into type the small amount of copy on the cards. An artist who works for the shop can draw simple figures that you might want as illustrations.

You could have the printing done on 3M "Post-it Notes" to make it easy to stick them to display cases, to cash registers and to counters without permanently marring surfaces. "Post-it Notes" are sticky on the back.

Or, print on pressure-sensitive adhesive labels in rolls. They can be peeled off easily so they won't permanently mar a business's property, either.

In these ways you can attract a lot of attention for a few dollars.

Another type of sticker can be used on envelopes containing your monthly payments. (Ask the print shop for suggestions.) These stickers can bear messages such as: "Letter Enclosed: Please NOTICE it." Or: "Credit Previous Payment, Please."

Here are examples of illustrated messages that one irate consumer printed on tent-shaped "mini-billboards" that she left at restaurants:

- "The Food Was Cold." (Illustration: Icicles hanging from a plate of food.)
- "One Could Grow Old Waiting For Service." (Illustration: Customer's long beard wound around a leg of the table at which he's seated.)

This is all perfectly harmless. Most employees have a sense of humor and will derive a sardonic sense of pleasure from the mini-billboards.

Don't ever put stickers on boxes of merchandise or on merchandise itself because doing so might delay sale of the merchandise. Your object should be to inform the business that it has unhappy customers and to give the business a hint of the reason for the unhappiness, *without* being destructive.

Instead of posting cards and mini-billboards around a business, you might want to hand them to service employees directly. Make steady eye contact as you do so. They will know that you are serious.

If you are going nowhere with front-line people, write on the backs of the cards: "TO: Store Manager" (or other appropriate title). Leave cards at customer service desks or checkout counters — or march into the executive office area and hand them to a receptionist.

Don't get carried away with this sort of activity, though. Be determinedly constructive. Criticize constructively.

The day a business discovers that customers have rights and begin honoring them is the day that you stop your propaganda campaign.

This is the same day, too, that the owners, managers, and other employees of the business should find you and give you a gift certificate for the favor you've done them. (We're only kidding.)

MORE GUERILLA TACTICS

If you've spoken to the salesperson responsible for your disgust, and if you've had a meeting with a manager, supervisor, or even with the president or owner; if you've called the business; if you've sent well-documented letters; and if you have only brush-offs and insults to show for it, then it may be time to bring up the heavy guns. Now may be the time for...*Guerilla Tactics*

Guerilla tactics are appropriate if you've been stonewalled by a company determined to prove that it is right, that you are wrong, and that it was nervy of you even to ask for correction of an error, for apology for an insult, for replacement of a product, or for your money returned.

Consider the following guerilla tactics or fashion your own creative variations. But, please note: Do *not* damage property. Doing so is illegal. You could be sued or charged in criminal court.

And keep in mind at all times that you are dealing with a throwback, a pariah in the business world, a business that's headed for financial trouble. Most businesspeople are your friends. They would never do anything to alienate you on purpose.

Bad service often is an oversight. Or an error. If you've never made a mistake, only then are you justified in condemning a business' every blooper.

RESTAURANT — A packed restaurant foyer is a dead giveaway that overbooking is business-as-usual here *or* that this is a very "hot" restaurant.

If you're kept waiting 20 minutes or so for a *reserved* table, what can you do besides telling the maitre d' that you don't intend to wait any longer? (Walking out isn't very satisfying.)

First ask the maitre d' if he will tempt the people loitering at the table reserved for you to leave by offering to buy them an after-dinner drink at the bar.

Here's another idea to try, but only if it fits your personality: Propose to the members of your group that each of them call in a reservation to the restaurant for the most popular seating time on the same evening. You agree among yourselves on the reservation night. Your friends will give assumed names. And you all agree that no one will show up.

The maitre d' will wonder what curse has been visited upon his restaurant. About a half hour after the time for which the reservations were made call the maitre d' and gloat.

Or, drop in on the nearly empty restaurant and accept immediate seating.

In restaurants, the best guerilla tactic, though, may be *no tip*...or an insultingly small tip. But, in America, restaurant patrons often are too embarrassed to leave a small tip or no tip. So, they tip even though service was insulting and slow. Their tip *reinforces* and *rewards* slow, insulting service, making it more likely that future patrons also will receive bad service.

The proper tactic is to tip generously — 15 to 20 percent — for good service. Consider pocketing tips that you do *not* give to a waitperson who gives bad service, saving it to give to the next waitperson who gives outstanding service.

Food critic Jeremy Iggers says: "I usually tip in the 15 to 17 percent range; but diners should base their tips on the quality of service.

"Bad service — when you can determine that the server is at fault — deserves a minimal tip, or none. When you receive exceptionally good service, especially at an inexpensive restaurant, it may be appropriate to tip more than 20 percent."

This business of undertipping is something that a lot of people hesitate to do because waiters and waitresses are good at tossing an insult at you as you leave.

But, be fair about it. Be sure that the poor service is not the chef's fault instead of the waitperson's fault.

HOME IMPROVEMENT CONTRACTOR — A contractor does some home improvement work for you and the workmanship is shoddy. Very shoddy. Water runs down your walls. But, your check has been cashed and the contractor is uncooperative.

Most contractors would "make it right," but this book is not written to help you in your dealings with legitimate, service-oriented businesses that appreciate your business and want you to return to buy again.

If you encounter an obstinate business that doesn't seem to care if it never sees you again, send a copy of an ad that you've had set into type, ready for placement in a newspaper.

The ad copy might read: "Have you had a problem with Jackal Construction Co.? If so, please call to discuss a class action suit against this contractor to seek substantial compensation for damages. (Your phone number.)"

You hope that the contractor sees the light after you show him the ad. You don't really want to spend the money to run the ad.

Unless you place the ad, you see, you haven't harmed the contractor, even though he deserves punishment for his incompetency and for his hard-headed obstinacy.

Some situations justify an "open letter" to the president of an offending company. Newspapers sometimes publish them in the "Letter to the Editor" section.

Send a copy to the president of the company with a note giving the date on which you'll mail the letter. Businesses cringe at the thought of negative publicity, so you may get satisfaction.

NEWSPAPER DELIVERY — One homeowner's daily newspaper seemed to end up in a puddle outside the door every time it rained. Even though the paper arrived in a plastic bag, he still resented the need to bend over and remove the paper from dirty water. After weeks of fuming and calling the newspaper's circulation department, the homeowner had a brainstorm.

He sent the next subscription check to the newspaper floating in a transparent plastic bag full of water, with a note explaining the significance of the unusual packaging.

Suddenly, prodded by the circulation manager, the newspaper delivery person discovered dry spots in which to drop the ingenious consumer's newspapers.

Another homeowner had a similar newspaper problem. The paper ended up in the bushes almost every evening.

So, the homeowner cut out the newspaper's ad promising front-door delivery, wrote a message on it, and sent it to the president of the newspaper publishing company.

The publisher didn't reply. But...surprise, surprise...the paper began appearing on the front step. Also, realizing the foolhardiness of making a promise they probably couldn't keep, the newspaper deleted the promise of front-door delivery from ads.

PAYMENT BY MAIL — A consumer couldn't get a response from a human being (just a computer) when she complained, as she did frequently, about a payment that the computer refused to credit.

So, she sent the company a check for $*000.00*.

A check for no dollars and no cents caught the attention of the computer. Now it was in the best interests of the computer's keeper to call the consumer. The call was made within a week.

Over the phone came the sound of an *un*recorded human voice. The consumer made her point, forcefully, and, voila!, the credit she had been seeking for months appeared on her next statement.

Nobody was hurt. The consumer was helped.

PICKETING; LEAFLETING

A Philadelphia consumer group, Consumers Education and Protective Association International, Inc., finds that more than 90 percent of complaints are resolved after a hostile and obtuse business is picketed — or after leaflets or booklets describing a problem with the business are distributed to passers-by or shoppers.

Picketing is more effective than leafleting in attracting public attention, and often media attention. But leafleting can present more detail about a complaint than is mentioned on picket signs, and a leaflet can be taken home and read.

Before setting up a picket or leafleting project, give the business plenty of opportunity to settle any service complaint. If you get no satisfaction and decide to proceed, here are several basic legal requirements to observe, in addition to local laws:

- ❑ At least one picketer or person represented by the picketers must have a genuine dispute with the seller.
- ❑ What pickets seek must not be unlawful, nor can the objective be closing of the business. It can be the resolution of a particular complaint or the changing of a specific bad practice.
- ❑ Picket signs must not contain false claims or exaggerations.

  For example, it is permissible to state that the car you bought from a dealer is a lemon and that the dealer refused to render satisfaction; but it is not all right to state that the dealer sells only lemons and always stonewalls his unhappy customers.
- ❑ Picketers may not use violence or abusive language or "breach the peace." Too many picketers or too much involvement with passers-by may be considered "breach of the peace."
- ❑ Picketers may not prevent people from walking on the sidewalk or entering and leaving the store.
- ❑ Location of picketing or leafleting should be related to its purpose. Demonstrating at the offending store is appropriate. Demonstrating at the owner's home usually is not appropriate.

Try to have a lawyer associated with your group. He or she should make sure that your group doesn't violate the law.

Notify police that you will be picketing/leafleting and that you have taken steps to make sure that you are not violating the law.

The purpose of these "guerilla" tactics (and you probably can come up with some prize-winning variations) is to call attention to poor service. When business is *aware* of bad service they will almost always take steps to stop it.

Whenever you walk the extra mile to inform a business that service stinks, you are making a personal contribution to a guarantee of good service that is the right of every consumer who spends money to help support a business and its employees.

CHAPTER 22

BLAME THE MACHINES

"Machines are great at acting,
but legions of consumers will swear,
they are incompetent when it comes
to reacting to anything but routine needs."

As *need* for service rises, the *amount* of personal service delivered declines. Why? Because business, preoccupied with short-term savings, turns over much service delivery to machines.

Let's look at voice mail systems, a perfect example of non-service. There's no service in voice mail for many customers, just for the sponsoring company. The telephone company benefits, too, because callers often end up making more than one phone call after reaching a dead-end and a disconnect, according to a study of these systems.

The manufacturer of this kind of equipment benefits, of course. The manager in charge of systems at the user company benefits also because he/she becomes a hero by saving much money in the elimination of human operators.

Finally, the personnel department benefits because the payroll declines.

The only *loser* is the customer who is put to a lot of trouble trying to complete a call. One waits 30 seconds for a recorded message and then another 30 seconds for another message before giving up.

Machines are great at *acting* but, legions of consumers will swear, they are incompetent when it comes to *reacting* to anything but routine needs.

When a transaction proceeds according to a computer program, then the machine purrs along smoothly.

But, when a consumer holds up a hand and says "That's not what I ordered" or "I don't want to know my balance, the amount of my last deposit *or* payoff amount" then the machine *still* purrs along contentedly...dumbly...unresponsively.

Of course, we can't blame the machines. The people who operate the machines are at fault. Service is only as good, as complete, accurate and fast as the people who run the machines.

Part of the blame must be accepted by business decision-makers, the bosses of the people who operate the machines. Often they add technology strictly for their own benefit. Or so it seems to consumers victimized by computers that dial their phones and then speak to them. ("Sequential dialing" phone equipment is used to reach more prospects at less cost, even those who have unlisted numbers.)

On the other hand, many companies are attracted to high-tech equipment by their *potential* to provide *better* customer service. That's a fact. That was the motivation for banks to begin installing teller machines on streets and in retail stores.

Still, some business executives act as if they are blinded by the glitter of technology. They automate to save money or to make more money — *not* to improve service to their customers. Not even to avoid a decline in the *present* level of service.

Often they don't stop to ask *the big questions*: *"How will this automated procedure affect our customers?" "Will their needs be met?" "What problems will this automation create?"*

Funds are transferred electronically. Robots take over from people on the assembly line. Computers do all the calculating and feeding information to printers that print invoices and account statements. Millions of transactions every day in insurance companies, banks, and other financial institutions are handled electronically.

But, business has failed to achieve customer comfort with the machines of the electronic age, a fact that diminishes their capability to deliver service.

A cartoon expresses the consumer predicament. It shows a man wearing an anxious expression standing belly-up to a curb-side teller machine. His expression says that he's hoping against hope that the gadget, over which he has no control, will dispense money from his account when he punches in the right numbers.

The cartoonist leaves us to wonder whether the machine paid off.

CHAPTER 23

HOW TO GET ROYAL TREATMENT EVERY TIME YOU BUY

"The Golden Rule:
Treat employees the way
you want to be treated."

Imagine service with a smile, employees who rush to help you quickly and to answer every question with certainty. Imagine *never* getting into hassles with employees or harangues with their supervisors.

One way to achieve this state of bliss is to patronize only businesses that provide fabulous service at all times. Since there aren't enough businesses like that to go around, take matters into your own hands. *Make* good service *happen*.

Let there be no doubt: You *can* do something yourself to improve the level of service that you receive.

Consider these means of making good service happen:

1. Change your attitude about service employees. Many employees were conditioned in the 1980s social climate to feel that it is much better to be the boss than the bossed. They believe, and they say: "Nobody tells me what to do!" They are proponents of the belief that the customer is always wrong in any encounter with a service delivery employee.

   To many of them service is sort of an insulting word. Providing service is demeaning. They are determined that they won't do one whit more for you than they must do to keep you from complaining to their supervisors.

   Now, understand that people are a product of their environments. They learned their values and behaviors from family and friends, from all the people they've come in contact with, and from prevailing social standards that they see acted out around them every day. So, be tolerant toward service people: They're just acting out their social conditioning.

   Set out to reeducate them.

   Sure, service people ought to rush up to you with a smile on their faces and say, "Is there anything I can do to help you?" But, if they don't, don't become angry. Try to influence their behavior. Even turn them into friends.

2. Act in a friendly manner toward service employees. A sales transaction basically is a social transaction. You earn good service the same way you make friends, by applying the Golden Rule. You receive in direct proportion to what you give. So, do this:

- ❑ Smile when you approach a service employee. Use good eye contact. Call the employee by name if you know it or if you can read it on a name badge. Greet the person with a friendly comment.

- ❑ Compliment employees on knowledge, helpfulness, dress, grooming...anything. One way to sustain good service is to tell a helpful or friendly or knowledgeable clerk that you appreciate their good service. Service people receive kind words so rarely that their memories of compliments and complimenters are very acute.

- ❑ Look pleasant. Don't scowl. Despite training, employees may hesitate to approach a customer who looks like he or she ate clam shells for breakfast. George LaMarca of Des Moines, whose occupation is handling disputes between consumers and businesses, gives an example of "the friendly approach" in action. He suggests that instead of yelling at a waitress about poorly cooked meat or cold hot apple pie, win her over with friendliness, even if you don't feel friendly. She'll carry your message to the chef and say something like: "There's a gentleman out there who's unhappy with his meal." That will get much better results for you than: "There's an old grouch out there who's been giving me an ear full..."

  If you treat employees brusquely and if you indicate by your manner that you feel that they are obligated to respond to your every outrageous whim, then you will receive the service equivalent of a chop to the solar plexus.

3. Ask for good service: "I really need your help. I don't know anything about VCRs" (or perennial flowers; or hiking boots; or boom boxes).

   Every human being loves to be asked for help. It makes them feel worthwhile. Needed. A request for help is a compliment, implying that you think that the person addressed is capable of helping.

   At Byerly's supermarkets in the Minneapolis-St. Paul metro area, every employee is required to answer every request or to write it down on a note pad that all employees carry, and to obtain the answer immediately from a supervisor.

   The supermarket chain's customer service reputation is so good that advertising, except by word of mouth, is unnecessary. The chain's only advertising (with a few inexpensive exceptions) is free — word-of-mouth recommendation by pleased customers. Is it possible that exceptional service has won this reputation for Byerly's?

4. Avoid asking questions endlessly and unnecessarily. Don't, for instance, ask price, sizes, colors, and so on when the information requested is prominently displayed on price tags or signs.

   Stories are told about people — male and female — who try on every shoe in a shoe store before buying. A consumer has a certain responsibility to know what she or he wants before asking a salesperson to sell it.

5. Act as if you expect good service, suggests Jane O'Brien of the Los Angeles Better Business Bureau. "The main thing," says O'Brien, "is to give salespeople the benefit of the doubt. Feel as if everything is going to go all right until it doesn't. "And practice the Golden Rule: Treat employees the way you want to be treated."

6. Dress neatly and cleanly.
   Just as people dressed like bankers get more respect than people dressed like The Three Stooges, so does a customer get more respect — and more attentive service — if he or she is dressed neatly in clothes without soup stains on them.

   The story is told in a Pittsburgh department store of a middle-aged woman who violated just about all the Rules for Royal Treatment By Salespeople.

   As she entered the Daywear department a look of anger spread over her face. It was as if someone was standing at the entrance with an invisible paint brush and swabbed the look of disgust on her face as she passed. Perhaps she was remembering past bad treatment. If so, she was assuring herself of more of the same.

   The lady wore a faded dress, muddy shoes, and a hair-do that looked like it was home to a family of wrens.

   She looked around and spied a clerk atop a stool, reaching high to place some boxes on an upper shelf. The clerk hadn't noticed the customer, yet.

The scowling customer walked to within 10 feet of the clerk and said, "Hey, you. Have you got time to wait on somebody today?"

She got exactly the service she deserved.

Customers are not always right, though some businesspeople exhort employees to act as if they are always right. Some customers don't know what they want and they also are overbearing, rude, and insulting.

Often these are the same customers who complain the loudest about poor service. It's a mystery to them why so many salespeople are...rude, overbearing, and insulting.

Another reason that people receive bad service is that they signal to clerks by their mannerisms, by eye and body movements, and by the tones of their voices that they expect service to be terrible.

Perhaps they can't be blamed for expecting poor service, though. The only good service they've ever known may have been provided by their mothers when they were children.

But, ask them if they would rather have service with a smile and eager salespeople who treat them like friends and they'll say, "Sure, but where do you find service like that?"

Maybe you don't "find" service. Maybe you make it happen. Force yourself to realize that you can do something about the level of service you receive. It is possible to get attentive, friendly service nearly all the time if you treat salespeople as friends.

If you change your attitudes toward salespeople, and if you act as if you expect good service, your chances of receiving good service improve immensely. A friendly attitude toward salespeople is so rare that clerks treated respectfully jump to attention and serve you as if you were a celebrity.

Chapter 24

WHAT'S IN IT FOR BUSINESS

"We can help these organizations see the light. That's good for us and for them."

Don't feel sorry for business, government, or non-profit groups when you complain about bad service. You're doing them a favor by complaining.

How else are they to know what causes customer or client dissatisfaction?

How else are they to stay in business except by satisfying complaints and by learning about the needs and wants of customers so they can *prevent* complaints — thereby generating the maximum number of *satisfied* customers possible?

Here are benefits of quality service for business, some of which also apply to government and to non-profit organizations:

1. Increase in market share and return on sales. Dominance in their markets.

2. More frequent sales. Repeat business. Larger sales. Order upgrading. Reordering.

3. More customers, including more new customers.

4. Savings in marketing-advertising-promotion budgets. When present customers remain loyal, companies don't have to spend as much money attracting new customers.

5. Fewer complaints. More word-of-mouth recommendation of the company to others.

6. Positive company reputation. This pays off both in attracting new customers and in making it easier to hire employees with customer service skills.

7. Differentiation from competitors. Often there's little difference among competitors in their products or merchandise. So, quality service becomes the reason that consumers choose one company over another.

8. Improved employee morale and productivity because customers respond positively to them.

9. Better employee communication: Staff members get along better together because they are in better moods, doing work they more often enjoy.

10. Fewer employee grievances, absenteeism and tardiness.

11. Less employee turnover. Lower retraining costs for veteran employees.

Here's a clear expression of the benefits of good customer service: Satisfied customers return. This is significant because 65 percent of the business of an established company, on the average, comes from customers that return again and again, according to the American Management Association.

When you complain, you can feel that you helped the business you complained to by prodding the company into better service.

So, feel good about complaining. You are doing a business, government, or non-profit organization a favor when you complain.

Some business, government, and non-profit organizations provide outstanding customer service. But, many others treat customers and clients as if they are obstacles or inconveniences instead of the source of their financial survival.

We customers and clients can help these organizations see the light. And that's good for us *and* for them.

If you have thoughts, comments or ideas about this book, I'd love to hear from you. (Please no requests for personal advice.) Write to me at the following address:

John Tschohl
Service Quality Institute
9201 East Bloomington Freeway
Minneapolis, Minnesota 55420 USA

Phone: (612) 884-3311
Fax: (612) 884-8901